PORTRAIT OF EAST HULL

MARY FOWLER

Highgate Publications (Beverley) Ltd.
1991

British Library Cataloguing in Publication Data

Fowler, Mary
Portrait of East Hull.
I. Title
942.837

ISBN 0-948929-53-7

Published by Highgate Publications (Beverley) Ltd.
24 Wylies Road, Beverley, HU17 7AP
Telephone (0482) 866826

Printed and Typeset by
B.A. Press, Tokenspire Park, Hull Road, Woodmansey,
Beverley, HU17 0TB
Telephone (0482) 882232

I would like to thank all the people who have shared their knowledge and memories of East Hull with me. I cannot mention all by name, but I want to record my particular gratitude to the following: Mrs. E. C. Anderson, Mr. J. Dempster, Mr. and Mrs M. J. Fenton, Rev. A. Harrison, Mr. J. W. Houlton, Mr. R. E. Kinns, Mr. K. Lowery, Miss A. M. Salvidge, Mr. E. Storr, Mr. H. R. Thompson, Mr. P. R. Townsend; Mr. G. E. Stephenson of Reckitt and Colman; staff at M & H (North East) Ltd.; staff at North Sea Ferries; the Secretary of Hull Kingston Rovers. I am also very grateful to my cousin, Mr. F. G. Kennedy, who drove me round East Hull to take photographs.

The picture of North Bridge (page 2) is reproduced by courtesy of Humberside Leisure Services. My thanks are due to Richmond and Rigg for their excellent photographic service.

Lastly, I wish to acknowledge the unfailing assistance of the staff of the Local Studies Library in Albion Street.

PORTRAIT OF EAST HULL

Most of East Hull as it stands today is a product of this century. Nineteenth-century beginnings are still to be seen, but vast areas of the city east of the River Hull are built up with Corporation housing estates, slum clearance of the 1920s and '30s with post-World War Two re-housing and expansion.

This book is an attempt to portray East Hull towards the end of the 20th century, with necessary glimpses of the past to make sense of the present. Change and decay were all around us a few years ago, but now the prospect is more pleasing. There is great variety: the stately pile of Holderness House (1838) and the charming bungalows of Rosey Row (1989); Buckingham Street (Board) School (1882) and Bransholme's Crystal Palace, the Perronet Thompson School (1988); the 14th-century brick and stone church in Sutton and the modern church of Mary, Queen and Martyr, at the edge of Sutton Park; small workshops in Drypool and the functional boxes of the Sutton Fields Estate; the busy container port at the Queen Elizabeth Dock and the new use of Victoria Dock as a housing development.

Old buildings still exist, but so often with modern additions and alterations that many East Hull people of an older generation have two mental images associated with the same building or view, one remembered and one as it is today. This is not a nostalgic essay, but a portrayal of old and new together, perhaps indicating, from changes that have already been made, what could happen in the future.

Not so long ago, the saying was that intrepid travellers coming into East Hull had to show their passports at North Bridge, thus describing more of the ignorance of Westerners than the isolationism of Easterners. It also gave importance to North Bridge as the entrance to East Hull. After a ferry service of centuries, the first bridge was built in 1541 as an adjunct to Henry VIII's extensive works at the Citadel. Not on the present site, but a little further downstream, Henry VIII's bridge was of stone and had six arches. Daniel Defoe on his visit to Hull in the 17th century, however, described North Bridge thus: 'They have a noble bridge here over the River Hull, consisting of fourteen arches' — an excessive number, it seems, as the river is narrow and would be virtually blocked by so many. Gent's illustration, from his 1735 *History of Hull* (shown over) is curious, depicting neither of the earlier-described crossings. It does show the Sugar House, numbered 12, built 1731 and standing, but dilapidated, in 1865. My mother had an expression for anything big and ugly: 'as big as Hull sugar house' which shows the persistence of folk-memory.

The old North Bridge, after major alterations in 1832 (during which bits of the 1541 structure were discovered) was replaced by Martin Samuelson's swing bridge of 1875. Its position can easily be seen, about thirty yards south of the present one. In the 1920s a new bridge was mooted and the line of the road was to be altered, together with the outfall of the Foredyke Stream. The present Schweitzer bascule bridge was opened in 1931 and some old property was demolished to make way for it. The picture was taken just prior to the closing of the 1875 bridge and the opening of the present bridge. By then, of course, several others were spanning the river, from the southernmost (Ha'penny Bridge from Humber Street to Garrison Side, then at the end of its working life) to the iron bridge further upstream at Stoneferry.

In 1990 and again in the summer of 1991, Scott Street Bridge was closed to road traffic for long periods. My picture affords an unusual view of the bridge's construction and also a glimpse of a wharf and industrial buildings on the east bank. It is a bridge of two parts, the east bascule being shown here. Each has a counterweight, seen below the timbers that are in the water, but if the bridge is lifted when the tide is high, the counterweights dip into the water and lose some of

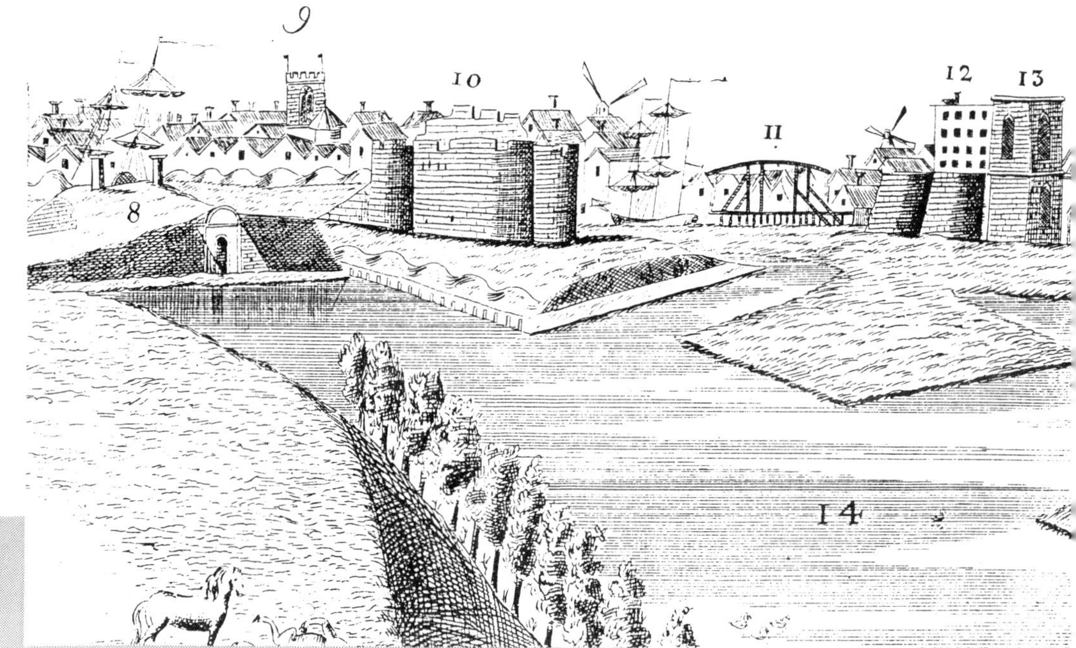

North Bridge (Gent).

The present and former bridges.

Reprinted with the kind permission of Humberside Leisure Services.

their effect because of buoyancy. The original 30ft deep well to the hydraulic main, connecting with a tunnel under the river and matched by a similar access well on the west side, is behind the short stretch of wall to the right of this picture. Granite stones on the west side near the bridge house show how long it took to build. At the top:

'City and County of Kingston-upon-Hull.
Scott Street Bridge.
This stone was laid by Alderman Wm Jarman,
Chairman of the Bridge Committee,
on the 3rd October, 1901.
Alderman W. A. Gelder, J.P., Mayor.
A. I. White, M.Inst.C.E., City Engineer.
E. Laverack, Town Clerk.'

Below the inscription on a smaller slab reads: 'The bridge was opened by Alderman William Jarman on the 3rd October, 1902'. Just one year.

John Ward's little painting of the river at Stoneferry with a large five-sail windmill on the east bank, looked upstream from about the present crossing to where the river bends. Hereabouts, at the beginning of this century, was a ferry which I have heard older people describe as an old man with a small boat. This postcard of the early years of the Stoneferry swing bridge, opened 1905, with the Bridgemaster's office, is looking towards East Hull and shows the chimney of Earle's cement works, demolished about 1930-31. This gentle scene became transformed with the advent of heavy lorries into a busy and hazardous bottle-neck. Many otherwise brave cyclists dismounted here and walked on the footway. In 1989-91 a new dual crossing was built, one bridge on the original site, the other a few yards upstream, necessitating the demolition of the old Premier factory and the Grapes public house. It is astonishing that the old bridge served heavy traffic for so long.

Pedestrians on the downstream walkway of the old Clough Road Bridge may have paused to admire this fine representation of the city's coat of arms in the ironwork. It was a large cartouche, maybe two feet high, and the surround of ropes, anchors and dolphins befitted the arms of a great port. The plaque was rescued by Mr. P. N. Robertson of Midgley and Sons, the demolition contractors, and presented to the County Council when the new bridges were officially opened on 23 July 1991. Now in the well between the two bridges, it is brightly painted to match the County Council's insignia on the opposite side, the only

decorations on the starkly simple and functional bascule bridges and where the old plaque seems much smaller than it did on the former, complex ironwork. Other bridges have their embellishments; for example, there are true lovers' knots in the ironwork of Chapman Street (Sculcoates) Bridge, 1875, and the present Drypool Bridge has a coloured plaque of an ancient sailing ship, but this was scratched and vandalised soon after the bridge's opening on 6 July, 1961.

The River Hull forms a natural western edge to this part of the city, but to the north and east Hull's shape and size have changed considerably, even in living memory. Beyond Noddle Hill Way there are still fields before the true boundary, the Holderness Drain, is reached. Castle Hill Road becomes a rough track between fields of rape and beans, with a curious tree'd mound ahead. This is Castle Hill, across the drain, just outside the city, once a destination for long walks or

adventurous cycle rides, for rumour had it that monks of long ago had a tunnel from Swine Church and reappeared as ghosts here. However, Tom Sheppard, excavating with a group of soldiers based at Sutton during the First World War, found a gravelly hill, with animal bones (evidently from food), 14th and 15th-century pottery fragments and the corner of a 16th-century brick building. So it was not a Bronze Age barrow, as some people had thought, nor Roman, even though Roman coins have been found hereabouts, but more likely a 'castle' of the 14th to 16th centuries. No evidence of monks and no ghosts!

Unnoticed by many who use the nearby bus stop, this marker is set in the kerbstone of James Reckitt Avenue, opposite Gillshill Road and near the back entrance to

East Park. It recalls the time when the Summergangs Dyke and Lambwath Stream were the northern boundaries of Hull. James Reckitt Avenue is just outside this old boundary, Summergangs Dyke being incorporated into the park and Lambwath Stream's bridge parapets still there near Malet Lambert School. In 1911 the County and Parliamentary boundary cut straight across open fields from this point to where Hantom Drain discharged into the Foredyke Stream (now at the drain bridge on Leads Road, Stoneferry) and Gillshill Road did not exist except as a cinder trod to Gillshill Cottage. This stone showed the limits of influence of the Hull Council and the Sutton Rural District Council.

It was not until 1900 that New Cleveland Street was cut through to the end of Witham where it met Bridge Foot, the old name of the length of road from Annison's to the former North Bridge. With New Cleveland Street came a new crossing of the Foredyke Stream or Sutton Drain. Although the drain is now filled in, the terracotta bridge parapets, constructed by the Accrington Brick and Tile Company at a cost of £112.12s. (£112.60), remain on each side of the road. Worked into the parapets are the three crowns of Hull and the date, 1903. There is also a metal plaque, recording the importance of this otherwise insignificant crossing: 'This bridge is the first built in ferro-concrete in Great Britain. Hennebique System. Constructed by Rose, Downs & Thompson, Ltd., Hull, in 1902.' The parapets have been cleaned in recent years, exposing a rosier hue to the now purer air than when they were covered with a patina of oily grime from the riverside factories. This picture was taken in 1968, five years before the Foredyke Stream was filled in.

The many drains excavated to dry out anciently marshy land in East Yorkshire and Hull were administered by Drainage Boards, committees responsible for maintenance of the drains. The banks on one or both sides of each drain were high with excavated clay, and occasional metal posts marked the limit of the Boards' responsibilities. Two uprooted posts of the Holderness Drainage Board were lying beside the fence of the Hedon Road Maternity Hospital in 1969. They will have long since gone, but this marker beside the filled in Foredyke Stream is firmly planted by the wall of Reckitt's Disprin factory, the 1911, building, the same site as a much older biscuit factory, burned down in 1866. There is also another marker now pushed deeply

into the grass verge of Marfleet Lane, near the drain bridge. Although rusted by a century of exposure, the date on each of them is clear enough: 1889.

John Smeaton, the builder of the Eddystone Light and of countless other lighthouses, harbours and bridges throughout the land, was here in November, 1763, surveying and making suggestions for the drainage of this part of Holderness. I took this picture of Marfleet Clough on 1 February, 1969, a dry cold day with a brisk north-east wind. At that time, Mr. Bliss was the keeper and one of his tasks was to keep the gates from being fouled by baulks of timber, etc. Just as well, for when I walked back along the bank, two lads were heaving a great beam into the drain from beside the old Withernsea line. Holderness Drain is still open. In parts the banks have been cleared to provide pleasant walks. At one time the water's edge was laced with water mint and meadowsweet in summer. It is still the resort of fishermen, as eels and coarse fish are to be found in the water.

Marfleet Clough.

At the end of Hopewell Road, with flat agricultural land beyond, the sluggish water of Flatty Dyke is clogged with the débris of civilisation. I have seen the dyke clean and free-flowing, but in May, 1991, when this photo was taken, it was a place 'where only man is vile'. I had not heard the name Flatty Dyke until the 1950s, even though I lived in Marfleet Lane, but as its real name is the Fleet or the Old Fleet, the translation into Flatty is quite understandable and much more descriptive than the original. The dyke or river had formed a boundary between Marfleet and Hedon, but now that Marfleet is part of Hull it forms the eastern city boundary.

Flatty Dyke.

Bridge parapets where there are no bridges are familiar sights in Hull, once intersected by many drainage channels and natural streams. Sources of disease, dumping grounds for rubbish through the centuries not merely in our own times, and too attractive to children for their own good, most of these watercourses have been filled in or culverted underground. Here on Ings Road is the parapet of Sutton Ings Bridge over the former Lambwath Stream, the section from Holderness Drain through the Ings Estate. The stream's course can be traced from here, through Malet Lambert grounds and behind James Reckitt Avenue

houses in the park, to a grassy area at the bottom of the south side of Summergangs Road, on its eventual, and now virtually lost, way to the River Hull. As a natural stream it was incorporated into the drain, but, as a watercourse itself, the major part of the Lambwath Stream now flows from Aldborough and through Skirlaugh to the higher reaches of the Holderness Drain.

Hull's links with Europe were made centuries ago in a two-way traffic that included marauding Norsemen coming up the Humber, trade with Hanseatic ports, regular sailings to Gothenburg, Hamburg, Rotterdam, Antwerp, Le Havre and elsewhere in the heyday of Hull as the third port in the kingdom, to the present trade of container vessels and North Sea Ferries. The Hull area has a sizeable population of Dutch immigrants and their descendants and both the landscape and the true dialect east of Hull have many features in common with those of our Netherlands neighbours. Our links with Rotterdam would therefore be obvious, even if William of Orange were not standing in the Market Place. The link with Freetown is through Hull's famous emancipator, William Wilberforce, and there is a maritime connection with Raleigh, U.S.A., in Operation Raleigh, based in Hull.

I dare say commuters coming in from Holderness barely notice this sign, but it (and others like it on other main roads) welcomes all comers to Hull, in this case at the Hedon Road city boundary.

From the end of the promenade in front of riverside houses on the Victoria Dock development, just before Alexandra Dock was re-opened, this was the eastward view of the city's most ancient and potent boundary, the Humber. Once this stretch of water was Victoria Dock's outer basin and the lock gates to the half tide basin are still to be seen. With buildings and equipment gone, this view emphasises the flat, low-lying nature of East Hull, most of it only a few feet above sea-level. Off right of the picture used to be the No. 1 Timber Pond and then Earle's shipyard, before Alexandra Dock was reached to the east.

It seems that there had been some sort of fortification on the east bank of the River Hull where it meets the Humber, since the middle 1300s, to provide security for one end of the chain which could be drawn across to seal the port. In 1541, Henry VIII visited Hull, regarded its defence as wanting and caused the building of a substantial castle on the east bank, partly on Crown land that had been acquired from Swine Priory, Thornton Abbey and the Carthusian Monastery in Hull, at the Dissolution. With the stability of eighteenth century government, the fortifications fell partly into decay, although the Citadel itself was used for military purposes into the middle of the last century. Factories and workshops sprang up in the southern part of Drypool and in 1890 the last surviving watchtower of the old Citadel was hemmed in by the Humber Iron Works. This is the South Blockhouse, showing the watchtower or bartizan, which was taken to East Park in 1912. It is now (October 1991) being

moved back to the Citadel site, to a more easterly position than it first occupied.

'Peter, Once quicksand man, then called
A rock; three times denied
The name who gave my name.
The moving ghost filled all
My shifting, made me firm.
Frank Redpath 6.12.87.'

Surmounting a plinth and the above inscription, St. Peter the fisherman sits firmly and pensively on the site of Drypool Church. It is a modern sculpture by Kevin Storch, put there in 1989, on the 50th anniversary of the outbreak of World War Two. More of the gravestones have been taken away; now only a few exist, propped against the western boundary of the area, but none of those which marked the graves of men who fought in the Crimea. St. Peter's Church itself, originally a chapel of ease in Swine parish, became a parish church in its own right as industrialisation brought increasing population to the district. Shift of population in the late 19th century as Holderness Road was developed, caused another change in Drypool's status, when St. Andrew's, Abbey Street, became the parish church of Drypool, with St. Peter's dependent upon it. This site was bombed and the ruins demolished to make a quiet open space, so that it is difficult to imagine it as the Garrison Church where the soldiers paraded on Sundays.

Little remains now to show that Drypool was once a village in its own right, for it was so close that it soon became absorbed into the spreading town of Hull, especially after the extensive work on the Citadel in 1541-3. During the early part of this century, there was still a 'village' community, living in old, rented property, some of the highest density housing in Hull at 84 dwellings per acre. Some clearance was effected at the beginning of the century when Clarence Street was pushed straight through from Drypool Bridge to Holderness Road, cutting Alma street and others in two. Deliberate slum-clearance between the wars removed much of the sub-standard housing, and, of course, 1940s bombing demolished still more,

indiscriminately. The off-licence at the corner of Prior Street had a cottage-y appearance because of its shape and its pantiled roof, but it has gone, and Prior Street also, since this photograph was taken in 1963.

This is the drawing of Sutton Church as it was in the 1830s, from Poulson's *History of Holderness*. The scene is still recognisable, as the curve of the road and houses flush to the opposite pavement are pretty much the

same in general appearance, despite a gap made by demolition in July, 1991. Deriving from a chapel of the early 12th century, the church of St. James the Great is built largely of brick, embellished with stone and with a long stone chancel. Most of what we see today (and in the Poulson illustration) is of the 14th and 15th centuries. A mention of a distant view of the church's 'white tower' by Thomas Walton in 1956 *(A Day on the Holderness Railway)* was made at a time when the tower and the south side of the nave were roughcast, as they had been since 1793. The plastering was removed from the tower about 1886 but the rest of the roughcast remained until after World War Two. Cuthbert Brodrick's alterations, especially to the roof, changed the church's appearance somewhat, but basically it stands as it has done for centuries.

Sutton has two Victorian Methodist Chapel buildings. The one in Church Street, registered for the Wesleyan congregation in 1860, proclaims its origins in the front stonework and continues in use, but the former Primitive chapel in College Street, at the top of Ings Road, has not been used for worship for many years and has long been the Masonic Hall. Both these big chapels replaced earlier ones: a Wesleyan 1812, a Primitive 1832. Thus, as well as its Church-goers, Sutton had substantial Non-conformist congregations

well before the major East Hull chapels were built, beginning with Kingston in Witham in 1841. All of the elaborate old East Hull chapels have gone, so these in Sutton stand as symbols of the district's Nonconformity and this one as an example of the kind of elaboration that was common in chapel architecture. It also serves as a reminder that Sutton became a desirable suburban residence for people of means long before the word 'suburbia' was coined in its modern sense.

Sutton churchyard has, in this flat region, a remarkable drop from its northern edge. A vista of farmsteads in

level fields with hawthorn hedgerows, spread out as far as Swine Church until 1970s and '80s extensive house-building took up much of the nearer farm land. The rise to the church is less noticeable from the southern side, although perceptible enough when cycling up Highfield. The ridge on which the church stands is Sutton's reason for existence, for, even in times of flood, being well above the general level of the land round about, it was also above the water. Wandering through the churchyard, I come upon the names of old friends, as the parish extends over a major part of the East Hull that I know best. Probably the churchyard's most famous occupant, his name perpetuated in a street near his home on Holderness Road, is Boswell Middleton Jalland, 'The Adonis of Holderness House', who kept the orange flag of Liberalism flying in East Hull for much of the last century.

The Elms is a double-fronted Victorian villa standing in a tree'd and shrubberied garden off Lowgate in Sutton. At the side of the house is a whalebone arch,

The Elms.

and this year the Sutton-in-Holderness Society added a small explanatory plaque which will no doubt be of interest to many visitors to The Elms, for the house is now a retirement home.

'Whalebone Arch. These jawbones of a Greenland whale were erected in the grounds of Sutton Hall, now demolished, belonging to Thomas Bell (1786-1851), oil merchant and owner of the whaleship HARMONY. Probably put here in 1820 when Capt. Sawyer returned to Hull with the product of eleven whales including nine pairs of jawbones....' Of the Greenland yards on the east bank of the river just north of Chapman Street bridge there is no trace, the Whalebone Inn is west of the river and so this arch is East Hull's reminder of the lucrative and horrible trade which flourished in the 18th and 19th centuries.

Sutton, unlike Marfleet and Drypool, has material reminders of the original village which only became joined to Hull when Gillshill Road and parts of Ings Road were built up in the inter-war period. Old names

such as Lowgate, Tweendykes and Leads Road are parts of a history traceable back to the Domesday Book. In living memory Sutton was a more isolated community than now, centred around the church and the chapels. There were the usual Holderness brick and pantiled cottages, but also many larger residences for merchants and persons of importance in Hull: the Bladons at the Hornbeams, Priestmans at East Mount, Robsons at Sutton House, Samuel Powell of the firm of Hammond's at Tilworth Grange, and so on. Now some of these houses are converted to other uses, but the tradition of Sutton as a place of residence for well-known people is carried on by Mr. John Prescott, Labour M.P. for East Hull, who has a substantial Victorian house there. The northern part of the parish was a plain dotted with ancient farms, their names re-appearing in the housing estates of the 1960s onwards: Noddle Hill, High and Low Bransholme, Spring Cottage, Soffham and Kirk's Farm. In the village itself is a wide range of domestic architecture, including this cottage in Lowgate.

Possibly the most ancient track in Hull, Sutton Trod, retains the old Norse name for a trodden pathway, a word that has all but disappeared from common speech in this locality. Sutton Trod is just a narrow way between trees, mostly hawthorn, as it emerges from Sutton and approaches the slope of the bridge over the old Hornsea line at Sutton Road. Beyond there it becomes a decent paved way behind modern houses, and peters out before Chamberlain Road is reached. I cannot find out when the name Sutton Trod began to be used. It was certainly before I was born, but neither does it appear on maps, nor does Blashill use it,

preferring the more prosaic and less descriptive word 'footway'. Sayer III, Lord of the Manor of Sutton in the reign of Henry III, granted this right of way, among others, to the nuns of Swine to enable them to reach Drypool. At that time, long before the Enclosures, it was probably an open track across marshy ground.

Joseph Armytage Wade, timber merchant, lived in Hornsea and it was largely due to him that the Hull-Hornsea line was opened in 1864, providing not only an outlet to the coast, but also a fast surburban link for Sutton village. After the Beeching cuts of the 1960s, the railway track was taken up and a good firm pathway made of parts of the line from the Swine side of Sutton station, under the 1863 road bridge (Close, Ayre & Nicholson, Phoenix Foundry, York) to Tweendykes, thence to Chamberlain Road and beyond. It is a haunt of blackbirds; a mild February afternoon will bring thirty or forty of them to a bushy spot close to the Sutton Road bridge in a kind of corroboree-prelude to the mating season. In places whitebeam and other

Former Hornsea railway line.

Former Hornsea railway line.

ornamental trees have been planted, but the dense natural hawthorn hedgerow, thorny and growing low to the ground, insulates the walker in a mini-countryside. The worst spoilers of this rural scene seem to be some local residents who dump garden rubbish (not open to rot, but in plastic bags) and other detritus of home and garden improvements. Sutton Road bridge is a vantage point in this flat land; Sutton Church, Beverley Minster, the Humber Bridge, Holy Trinity, the Guildhall and the North Sea Ferry at her berth are all visible from the top. Also the new sails of Rank's old mill may come into view when the East Park trees lose their leaves; it is too early to tell.

Once a view over a village scene, with the flat fields of Holderness relieved only by the towers of Preston and Hedon churches, the vicinity of Marfleet's old station on the Withernsea line is changed to a semi-industrial area that unsuccessfully tries to hide behind the former hedgerows and trees. The railway line is long since gone, but the station house of that curiously distinctive ordinariness of all railway houses, stands as a reminder of trips to 'Witherunsea', a favourite venue of East Hull people, when buses and trains were frequent and cheap and two stations, Southcoates as well as Marfleet, served the eastern part of the city.

Former Withernsea line, Marfleet.

Barely out of earshot of heavy lorries, St. Giles' Church, Marfleet, is in a secluded corner of an old village now overwhelmed by docks and industry. It was a predominantly agricultrural area until the late years of last century, when Alexandra Dock crept up to its western boundary, the Holderness Drain, and when Fenners established their works and built houses for their employees. St. Giles' Church, the third on this site, was built in 1884 to replace a church designed in 1793 by George Pycock, the architect of the old Hull Royal Infirmary. Various monuments from Pycock's building were put into the present church as they were

all comparatively recent, the former church being less than a century old. Much of the internal woodwork is more modern, some of it the work of a local woodcarver, Mr. Clifford Longley. Now St. Giles' is part of a team ministry, centred at St. George's Church, Marfleet Lane (Sutton Trust), and including St. Philip's at the Barham Road-Amethyst Road junction of Bilton Grange and St. Hilda's on Annandale Road, Greatfield.

When this simple chapel was built for the Wesleyans in 1872, it stood on the former turnpike road to Hedon on

the eastern edge of Marfleet village, backed by marshy growths to the Humber bank. It was replaced by the chapel on Marfleet Avenue before the First World War, as this old building was de-registered as a place of worship in 1906, the new chapel built in 1908 and registered in 1913. Since that time, this building has served a variety of purposes or had periods of abandonment (as in the 1960s), but is now used as a workshop. King George Dock was excavated behind it and the more recent buildings of Anglia Oils etc. almost belie any idea that this once could have been a little rural chapel.

Moved from a more prominent position in Marfleet Avenue, the marble memorial to the killed and injured in the First World War is still intact. Few street memorials remain in Hull, as they were often in the form of glass-fronted shrines and although they were kept clean and supplied with flowers for twenty or so

years, come the Blitz and many were destroyed or damaged and the local population dispersed. A curious triangular stain on the brickwork at the top of Nornabell Street, Holderness Road, marks the position of that street's memorial, a more fragile thing than this marble plaque at Marfleet. In the 1920s, when the carnage of 1914-18 was fresh in people's minds, small open air acts of worship were conducted by the clergy of St. Andrew's Church near the memorials of the nearby streets. In those days each street was like a village; blank walls at the ends of terraces often shut off the next street from all communication, and, human nature being what it is, there was possible rivalry about the beauty and repair of each memorial, in loyalty to the 'lads' of the particular street.

Although Marfleet was taken into the town boundary in 1882, it was still an agricultural village, little more than a scatter of farms around the church. When Crowle Street School was opened by Hull School Board in 1884, Marfleet children had to go there and my guess is that many of them walked. The School Board built Marfleet School in 1892, just in time for an increase in population, as in 1890 the Fenner brothers had bought an 18-acre site, a former dairy farm, for their new factory which opened in 1893. The school still flourishes as Marfleet's Primary School and will be celebrating its centenary next year.

Long ago, Southcoates was almost a hamlet in its own right, although part of Marfleet parish. Southcoates Lane is an old thoroughfare and until it was built up between the wars, had ditches or streams running beside it. As in other parts of East Hull, there were windmills, farms and market gardens in Southcoates. Here in about 1894, Moses Salvidge stands with his family in front of their farmhouse, which many years later was pulled down to allow Preston Road to be constructed at the start of the building of East Hull Estate. The front windows looked out to where Southcoates Lane School would be built in 1912, but one of the windows is bricked up to reduce the window tax, a clue which probably takes the date of the building back into the 18th century. Although a dairy farm, a fair amount of rhubarb was grown here, Mr. Salvidge and a young son harvesting the crop very early in the morning and getting it to the docks by about 6.30am for shipment to Germany. Rhubarb growing was quite common in East Hull, down Westcott Street, and in Stoneferry particularly, but why any of it should have been exported to Germany is a mystery to me.

A charity school existed in Southcoates from 1856 to about 1909 as a result of the 1713 will of Eleanor Scott. The invested rents from a small farm and some land were used for over a century for a variety of poor relief and then in 1855 the school shown over was built on land now occupied by bungalows on the north side of Telford Street where it joins Southcoates Avenue. The schoolmistress was paid £30 a year and Miss Coates, seen here on the right, had that responsibility in the early years of this century up to the closure. As far as I know, it was always a one-teacher school, so I cannot say who the other lady was. £20 per year from the rents was diverted, partly to the Drypool National School and partly to the Dansom Lane British School because 40 children from the district were taught free in these establishments. After closure of the Southcoates school, some of the income was transferred to St. Peter's School, Drypool, and some of it provided Miss Coates with a pension. Southcoates Lane Council School opened soon after, in 1912. That was before East Hull Estate was started, and the first pupils walked from Summergangs Road, Lee Street and Newbridge Road to and fro, dinnertimes included, even infants of 5 years old.

Salvidge's farm.

To some passers-by, perhaps, these are just some more old people's bungalows, but they are in fact the almshouses built in 1934 from the proceeds of sale of some of the land left by Eleanor Scott in her will of 1713. East Hull has quite a share of endowed almshouses: those in Sutton's College Street, through the benevolence of Ann Watson; Ferens' Haven of Rest (1911) on Holderness Road and flats on Barham and Staveley Roads, and, since the 1980s, in Craven Street; the Frank Finn homes off Southcoates Avenue, not far from where Eleanor Scott's Charity School was; and houses originally provided by members of the Reckitt family, the Frederic Reckitt Homes and Juliette Reckitt Haven of Rest, both on Laburnum Avenue and the Sir James Reckitt Village Haven, also in the Garden Village.

East Hull's first industry was corn milling, and across the sparse flat landscape many windmills would have been seen during the last century, some of them changing to steam power (with a chimney and black smoke) as time went on. There were 11 corn or oil mills on Holderness Road to the present city boundary, only one of them, now the Cornmill Hotel, Mount Pleasant, a steam mill from the first (1838). There were several mills in Drypool, others in Hume Street, Craven Street, Southcoates Lane, Sutton and Stoneferry and also in Dansom Lane, including the giant Subscription Mill. This is Dale's mill, on the left of Dansom Lane, a little way beyond Pemberton Street. It was in open fields in 1814, but the houses and gardens of Pemberton Street, Pennington Street and Holborn Mount had crept up to it by 1848. Urbanisation and industrialisation of the riverside and its hinterland went on at increasing pace after that, and many of the firms that continued into modern times were based on two factors, imported seeds and milling. Over the years there has been the milling of corn, cocoa beans, castor oil seeds, palm kernels and other exotic seeds, spices and mustard as well as of rapeseed and linseed, etc. from which other products, notably paint, soap,

margarine and cattlecake were made, every factory pouring out stench and smoke into the air. Bombing badly depleted the riverside, as most of the raw materials and products were inflammable. Milling, nowadays, is a far less important part of Hull's industry than formerly, as many of the seeds are crushed in their country of origin, and oil, instead of seed, exported. Dale's mill stood well into this century and therefore is remembered by some older people in East Hull.

In front of the previous Windmill Inn was Albion Place, connecting with Naylor's Row. Until the end of the last century, instead of the wide triangular road junction, small buildings lined Holderness Road from Witham. The Blockhouse Mill was set back in the yard behind the present redbrick building with the wrought iron 'dome', Jackman's mill was near Blyth Street, and Tinegate's mill next to the Windmill Inn. Then a lot of old property was pulled down to make way for Clarence Street, a direct route from the Old Town to Holderness Road. About the same time (1902-ish), the Windmill Inn was rebuilt and a fine facade it presents. It is somewhat ironic that the legacy of a breed of largely Non-conformist Victorian millers should be a series of public houses on Holderness Road, but there they are: the Windmill with its wonderful tilework, the Cornmill, retaining some of the old features in its structure, and The Mill, cottages and windmill complete. That's conservation.

Painted black and with an advert. for Wilcox's stout at 2/6 (12½p) on the side, the tower of John Rank's windmill stood on Holderness Road, opposite East Park, like an old soldier: it would never die, only fade

away. The adjoining cottages where John Rank's grandson, Joseph, was born on 28 March 1854, and where, after the Rank family left, Slater Eyre lived into this century, have been in some sort of occupation ever since. There was Mrs. Coates, the fruiterer, and latterly the first cottage was a coal office. Mercer and Bowen, the monumental masons had the front yard for many years and some people will remember Mr. Houltby who mended bikes in the ground floor of the mill in the 1940s and '50s. The cottages were officially Eyre's Cottages for the best part of a century, but the fame of Joseph Rank was so great that everybody called it Rank's Old Mill.

Photo: courtesy of Mr. E. Storr

All of a sudden, it seemed, the mill cottages were restored, the yard cleared and reset with cobbles and the mill tower repainted so as to obliterate the advertisement. A new public house came into being: The Mill. Outside, the general appearance was retained. Inside, walls were taken down between the low ceiling'd cottages to make a bar-room, and a long narrower section furnished with settles and stools. Not over-decorated, it therefore has the ambience of a comfortable old inn, although I fear that the atmosphere may become oppressive under the low ceilings when the place is full. Then, during the morning of 18 June, this year, quite by chance I was taking photographs on Holderness Road and witnessed the placing of the cap on the mill and as there was also a fitment to take sails, the next step of restoration was not unexpected. By the middle of July the skeleton sails were added and Holderness Road once more has a windmill.

When Joseph Rank started in business on his own, he rented Waddingham's mill on Holderness Road, not far from Holland Street, then West's steam mill, now the Cornmill Hotel, before building the Alexandra Mill in Williamson Street in 1885. The culmination of growth of the firm in Hull was the Clarence Mill complex, begun in 1890 and extended during that decade by the addition of a further mill and a silo, filling a large site on the eastern river front on both sides of the road leading up to Drypool Bridge. The postcard view, looking up-river with the old Drypool Bridge open to let a tug pass through, shows the curve of the wharf south of the Drypool Basin, the river entrance to Victoria Dock, and the towering red-brick Clarence Mill on the extreme right. The mill was

bombed in 1941 and grain cascaded into the river, where it smouldered for weeks. The firm's operation in Hull is now restricted to the post-war mill at the south side of Drypool Bridge. Vessels come up the river to the wharf outside Clarence Mill and unload there, but of course the firm is now not just Rank's, but Rank Hovis McDougall. Across the road, where the rest of the Clarence Mills complex was, are now the related companies, the Gamebore Cartridge Co. and Shotwell Ltd., the tall building of which conceals a shot tower for the age-old process of making lead shot by dropping molten lead from a great height.

When Victoria Dock was formally opened on 5 July, 1846, the first vessel to enter was the Trinity House yacht, crowded with Trinity House boys. The last time I saw Victoria Dock in use, it was providing a berth for a single vessel, an ocean-going yacht, The Prospect of Whitby, and the Drypool Basin was a convenient place for Sea Scouts to sail a boat on a Sunday morning. That was 1969. The dock was filled in fairly soon after and a lot of its 'furniture' removed. The old power house, No. 9 Hydraulic Station, is still standing at the west end of the dock site, but of other buildings, nothing is left. At the end of last century, the principal use of Victoria Dock was the import of timber, seed, nitrate of

Photo: courtesy of Mr. E. Storr

Power House, Victoria Dock.

soda and guano, the latter the forerunner of the many kinds of fertiliser on sale today. I suppose organic growers would approve of it, as guano was a natural product, the accumulated droppings of countless sea-birds, quarried on islands off Peru and exported largely from Callao, a Peruvian port just north of Lima and, at 12° South of the Equator, probably one of the nastiest ports on Earth during the heyday of this type of trade. Neither was the Foreign Cattle Depot of Victoria Dock, on South Bridge Road, a place for congenial work. With accommodation for 600 head of cattle or 3,000 sheep and pigs, slaughterhouses for different animals, including one in which eight beasts could be slaughtered simultaneously, it was one element which made up the trade of the Third Port.

Thousands of men 'worked on the docks' in some capacity or another: those on the ships, on the dockside, and in the warehouses, all involved with the loading and unloading of cargo, each with his own expertise. There were skilled men needed for the running and maintenance of the docks and in the ship-building and ship-repair industries as well as many general labourers. This postcard is from the turn of the century, some years after the important seven-week dock strike of 1893 and thus at a time when there was a

high proportion of non-union labour among the workforce. Whatever the job, the work was hard: mechanical bulk handling was still in the future and heavy bags had to be humped from place to place. The lighters are gathered round the cargo ship in this picture and the position of the wharf may be judged from the conical tower of the prison seen above the sheds on Alexandra Dock side. Alex's trade was, in its heyday, dominated by the import of timber, much of it from Russia, and the export of coal. Fruit and oilseeds were also major imports and as seen here, overside discharge on to lighters was the chief method of handling this kind of cargo.

This photograph, taken on 22 May, 1991, records the end of a nine-year phase in the existence of Alexandra Dock. A single cormorant preened itself on a post in the middle of the dock, while men in curious little capsules were practising their use as, I presumed, unsinkable lifeboats. Where there had been molasses tanks until the Blitz, opposite the prison, was a bank varied enough in its vegetation for a nature walk, most of the railway lines had gone and some of the buildings removed or fallen into disrepair. When it first opened in 1885, Alex was, at 46 acres, by far the largest Hull dock. It cost in excess of £1,300,000 and with deep anchorage of 34′6″ (a level maintained by water pumped in from Holderness Drain) it could accommodate larger ships than hitherto. In comparison with the original cost, Associated British Ports spent £1,500,000 to restore the dock for its re-opening on 16 July 1991. On that day, 106 years exactly since the dock's original opening, a Russian vessel, the

7000-ton *Pioneer Yakutii* bearing a cargo of timber, was the first ship to enter the dock again on a trading basis. The reasons for re-opening Alex are embedded in Hull's hopes of greater participation in European traffic in 1992 and after. More berthing and warehousing space will be needed if recent upward trends in the port's trade are to be accommodated, and so the old dock has been brought back into use.

Two graving- or dry-docks were at the north-east corner of Alexandra, this one the larger of the two. The stone stairway to the floor of the dock, even on the dry day when I saw it recently, appeared treacherous, but someone who knew it in use in all weathers told me it was indeed a slippery access where care had to be taken, especially when carrying a heavy load. A pump house used to be close by, to take the water from the two docks, either singly or both at the same time.

Photo: courtesy of Miss E. Barnes

Graving Dock, Alexandra.

King George V opened the dock which bears his name in June, 1914, just before the First World War. Some time during the dock's seven-year construction period young Edith Barnes was taken by her parents to see what progress was being made and this photo is a memento of their visit. The dock was the most easterly and largest in Hull, at 53 acres, built as a joint effort by the North Eastern Railway and the Hull, Barnsley and West Riding Junction Railway and Dock Company. King George Dock handled general cargoes, coal and timber at different quays with facilities at No. 11 Quay for wet dock repairs. Elevators took grain directly into the silo, which was enlarged by half as much again in the early 1960s as grain imports had increased. Coal exporting declined in the 1950s, so alterations were made to accommodate the still buoyant trade in general cargoes. The large Wool Transit Shed was used after 1957 to house wool when dockside sheds were full. With the 1970s dock labour problems came the emergence of other, smaller harbours as ports in their own right, coinciding with the period when container handling became of paramount importance. This traffic is now dealt with at the Queen Elizabeth Dock, opened by Her Majesty in 1969.

The modern ferries plying the Hull-Rotterdam and Hull-Zeebrugge routes are ocean liners unlike the old *Bury*, *Melrose Abbey* and *Bolton Abbey* which preceded them. The older boats came into Humber Dock where customs and other formalities were dealt with in the draughty ochre-painted sheds lining the dockside. This is the *Norland*, famous as a hospital ship during the Falklands war of 1982-3, and lengthened and refurbished in 1987, so that now she can accommodate 889 passengers and 500 cars or 179 twelve-metre freight trailers. One of four vessels on the two routes, for passengers and freight lorries, the *Norland* (with the *Norstar*, *Norsun* and *Norsea*) is part of the success story of North Sea Ferries. 'Why drive south?' indeed when four comfortably equipped 'cruiseferries' are available and the terminal on King George dock is palatial in comparison with the former facilities. For the crews, too, the job is different from the older boats. A spacious

Photo: North Sea Ferries

bridge is not only equipped with modern instruments for navigating the vessel, but also with a bank of close-circuit T.V. screens to monitor what is happening in vital parts of the ship itself.

Off the north side of Hedon Road well beyond Marfleet, is a timber yard, one of Hull's oldest firms in its origin. Now trading as M & H (North East) Ltd., one of the long sheds of timber bears the earlier name: Richard Wade, Sons & Co. This type of shed used to be common in East Hull because of the number of woodyards: a huge black barn, the sides of well-spaced timbers to allow air to circulate within. Richard Wade came to Hull about 1780, already a businessman, I presume, for he appears in the *Directory* of 1781 as 'shipowner and timber merchant'. The family connection — son Abraham Wade, grandson Joseph Armytage Wade, etc. — continued, the firm expanded beyond Hull and flourished throughout last century. After the First World War a series of take-overs and mergers brought Richard Wade, Sons & Co. Ltd. under the control of May and Hassell in 1928, a member of the Wade family continuing in the firm until 1945. I walked round part of the 23-acre site and it brought back images of the many woodyards and sawmills of East Hull and of high-piled timber, pit-props and scaffolding poles behind the dock fences of Hedon Road. My father was a joiner, and some of my most potent memories of childhood are the smells of different kinds of wood. There is yet another interest in this firm, for the daughter of Joseph Armytage Wade became the second wife of Samuel Plimsoll, M.P. for Derby, the marriage solemnised in Hornsea Parish Church, 8 October, 1885.

In 1968, the date of this photograph, the Plimsoll's Ship Inn on Witham was still a going concern after 150 years as a public house. It had a period of neglect when

it was closed in the mid 1980s, but was carefully restored by Mansfield Brewery and re-opened in 1987. By then the next-door building had been pulled down and evidence of the existence of Union Court, the alley leading to the back of the Plimsoll, taken with it. The inn was most likely established about 1814 as The Ship and by 1830 the Union Court access was important as there was stabling for 20 horses. In 1876 it was bought by Gleadow and Dibb's Anchor Brewery, and because there were two other Ship signs in Witham (a road exceedingly well provided with pubs) the name was changed in honour of Samuel Plimsoll, 'the sailor's friend', whose Merchant Shipping Act was passed that year. Shipowners' unscrupulous practice of using 'coffin ships' to gain insurance money when the ships sank, was, by Plimsoll's Act, made illegal; owners had the duty to make sure their ships were seaworthy. The familiar Plimsoll Mark on a ship's side is part of the preventive measures to be taken against over-loading.

Entering the River Hull is a treacherous business, as I witnessed minutes after taking this photograph one summer evening. A Whitaker tanker, from Immingham possibly, was coming in at fairly low tide and the current took the craft broadside to the west bank near the pier where I was standing. The operation was, of course, successful, but the skill of manoeuvring these long vessels from the stern cabin must be quite considerable. The spit of land on the east bank is called Sammy's Point where now the Humber Conservancy Board have a yard containing variously shaped, brightly painted river buoys. In the middle of last century when the Citadel was at least partially dismantled, the land up to the point contained the shipyard of Martin Samuelson. He was described by the *Hull Free Press* at the time as having dark eyes and black bushy whiskers; white hat, blue coat and light trousers; who bowled along like an express train; in whose expression there was 'more of energy than dignity'; and his business was 'of utmost importance to the prosperity of the town.' The business was iron ship-

building, the time contemporaneous with the start of Earle's shipyard, but Samuelson's, after a flying start, did not last so long. The yard was taken over by Bailey's Humber Iron Works, but Hull had already coined the name, Sammy's Point.

In April, 1973, this old factory that had latterly been used by the C.W.S. was pulled down, thus removing the last tangible evidence of a Victorian enterprise. Realising that Hull exported cotton yarn, some local entrepreneurs thought that it could be produced here

more cheaply than in Lancashire. During boom years of the late 1830s and early 1840s two mills were established, one in Cumberland Street and this one, the Hull Flax and Cotton Mill, in the Groves area of Cleveland Street near the river. The works were extensive and for a short time before being superseded by Marshall's mill (the 'Temple of Karnak') in Leeds, boasted the largest room in the world. The Wesleyan Methodists held one of their centenary celebrations in the mill, which was barely finished at the time. The cotton enterprise foundered in 1857 and, although it was revived, finally ended in 1866. Many of the operatives had been children working half time and the Church of England built St. Mark's School close by in 1840 to cater for them, four years before St. Mark's Church was opened.

When Edward, Prince of Wales, came for a two-day stay in Hull, 12-13 October, 1926, he laid the foundation stone of the Ferens Art Gallery and toured a number of works, including Reckitt's. His hour-long visit there had been carefully planned to show him as many aspects of the company's activities as possible, with the workforce of about 4,000 assembled to greet him. Here the Prince pauses before the War Memorial in Dansom Lane, standing apart from the civic dignitaries with Mr. Arthur B. Reckitt, the Chairman of the Company, and Mr. T. R. Ferens. The Lord Mayor, Cllr. Frank Finn, J.P., and the Sheriff, Cllr. G. H. Jefferson, to the left of this picture, are identified by the chains of office, while the Deputy Lord Mayor, Cllr. A. Digby Willoughby, stands with his grey Homberg hat in his hands. Mr. Arnold Reckitt and Mr.

Gilbert Reckitt are also in the group. The social and welfare concerns of the company were not omitted from the Prince's tour; a swimming display was in progress when His Royal Highness visited the Baths and he was pleased to learn that the water had the chill off it.

Many internationally-renowned products have come from Reckitt's East Hull factories. Young people will not be familiar with Zebo black lead grate polish, nor the repetitious hard work that was put into cleaning the old black metal grates and stoves. Many people will remember that 'Out of the blue comes the whitest wash' and the posters of billowing white clouds and billowing white washing on the line against an ultramarine sky, advertising Reckitt's Blue. Very few, however, have not used Dettol, an antiseptic which came on to the market in 1933, first only for hospital and medical use and then on general sale. Here, about 1935, some of the hundreds of 'Reckitt's Girls' are at work in the Dettol plant. It is of interest to note that the

Photo: courtesy of Reckitt and Colman, Mr. G. E. Stephenson, Business Intelligence Unit.

building seen here, on Dansom Lane, was used as a hospital by the Voluntary Aid Department (V.A.D.) during the First World War. 'Almost every East Hull person either worked at Reckitt's or knew someone who did,' someone said to me recently.

I daresay that Joseph Henry Fenner, who had been in Hull for about 30 years when the original high level railway to Alexandra Dock was built in 1885, would have been gratified to know that well over a century on, a later railway bridge over Hedon Road would be forming a sign post to the extensive factory bearing his name. Brought up in a middle-class family that had been in the tanning and leather-dealing business and married to Elizabeth, daughter of the proprietor of Holmes' tannery, Joseph Henry Fenner nevertheless started his own business in a very small way in Bishop Lane in 1861. The first ten years were not easy, but in the early 1870s he took larger premises in Chapel Lane and was increasingly concentrating on leather strapping that was pre-stretched to run true when attached to a machine. By the mid-1880s the business was well established, but the founder died after being thrown from his horse and trap in the spring of 1886 and it was left to his sons, Harry and Walter, to carry on. They made a leap forward in 1893 by building a factory on the outskirts of Hull, on a large site, not fully utilised until after World War II. Still on the Marfleet site, but much extended since, it is surrounded by houses, many of which Fenners built for their workers.

There were plenty of small firms in East Hull, of course, each employing a few people. In the 1920s and '30s H. Gill and Sons were undertakers operating from 344, Holderness Road. It is evident from this advertisement postcard that they supplied wedding cars also. The car is on Holderness High Road about opposite Marfleet Lane, showing the rural nature of that district before Ings Estate was built. It prompts me to add another picture, taken perhaps a hundred yards from the other; here Paddy stands ready for any adventure, at the end of the ten-foot way next to No. 748 Marfleet Lane in 1927. The background is of more interest than the dog: the corner of St. Michael's Church (consecrated that same year, 1927), no vicarage, and long before the semis were built, a haystack and the end of the cowshed belonging to a small farm which was there until 1945. I heard recently that St. Michael's first incumbent, the Rev. Reginald Newcombe, arrived here by 'plane, but whether or not he landed on these very fields, I cannot tell.

Reed's Lane, the rough track from Southcoates Avenue to the bottom of Aberdeen Street, was an unnamed field path at least a century ago. Southcoates Avenue's houses were built 1910-ish from the Holderness Road end. The bakery at the corner of the track and the Avenue was a going concern by 1912 and there were already several shop outlets in Reed's name, supplied by an earlier bakery in Cleveland Street. The name of the track, therefore, derives from the bakery and is no ancient name signifying a marsh or similar. The bakery workers posed for this photograph in 1921, showing another East Hull firm providing work for a few men and women. Reed's amalgamated with Mackman's and expanded so that there were shops of Reed and Mackman in different parts of the City.

Later, the 'Reed' element in the name was dropped and the shops were known as J. J. N. Mackman Ltd. McLeish's and Skelton's are now the household names that Reed and Mackman used to be. All is change. A pleasant enough pathway beside well-kept allotments has become an unwholesome track with the disuse of the gardens. Where once one could buy fresh produce, now the allotments are filled with rubbish and modern dwellings have replaced the bakery. Such was Reed's Lane, mid-1991. In September, a compulsory purchase order was served on the allotments and a development of houses, Salvation Army centre, a church, and some kind of health or community centre are proposed, leaving part of the area clear for recreation.

Taylor's Laundry in Southcoates Lane provided work for both men and women for a long period and then was taken over by Bentley's, continuing until the disastrous fire in September, 1990. On the south side of the lane, it stood opposite the market gardens on which Savery Street and Watt Street were built. T. S. Taylor, the laundry's founder, lived in the villa, 'Cleveland', next door to it and was an active Liberal. He was Mayor at the time of King George V's Coronation, 1911, and these pictures of Cllr. and Mrs. Taylor appeared in the souvenir booklet presented to Hull schoolchildren. Mrs. Taylor stands slightly nervously in her finery before Turner and Drinkwater's camera, her dress, sumptuous though it is, presaging the simplicity of line which would follow after the war. Taylor advertised

TAYLOR'S LAUNDRY LTD.

Art Dyers . Dry Cleaners . General Launderers

Curtain and Carpet Cleaners. **Shirt and Collar Dressers**

Unequalled for Quality of Work and Service for Seventy Years.

Your enquiries are invited about our "FLOAT-IRONED" Service, and our "IPAC" Repairing Process.

SOUTHCOATES LANE, HULL.

Telephone 31896 (2 lines).

regularly in a number of places, this one being taken from the *Trinity Church Monthly*, the Coltman Street Wesley Circuit Magazine for 1911, thus showing that his trade spread to other parts of the town. Even working people used the laundry for one important item: men's stiff collars. Last year's fire destroyed the washing and drying area and now Bentley's have a new plant in Harrow Street, Hessle Road, operational from 19 August 1991.

The flats at Regis Court and Jalland Lodge are built on what was formerly a claypit and brickworks, one of many in East Hull. This one was worked out by the early years of this century, but there was another, round the corner of Marfleet Lane up to the drain which continued into the 1950s. The choking sulphureous smoke densely fogged the roadway when the wind was in a certain direction. On Monday, 5 May 1913, the *Hull Daily Mail* carried the following description of the Regis Court site: 'Marfleet Lane from the Holderness Road forms a delightful pastoral

walk .... Many who favoured the walk yesterday were surprised to find that the familiar brick pond had been converted into an ornamental lake with rockeries constructed and the banks covered with shrubs and trees now full of foliage. In the middle of the lake there is an island. There were two swans enjoying the beauty of the scenery and making themselves quite at home. It struck me that the lake would be an ideal resort in the hot summer months, for I saw already there two boats and I am told that the water is well stocked with fish.' Remnants of these delights existed when I was a child and it was one of those semi-forbidden places to linger on the way home from school. Barely a sign of the brick industry remains in East Hull, apart from the many houses that were built of the local product. The other Marfleet Lane brickworks was filled in and levelled and now Winchester Avenue and Close are there; the site had been considered by Hull Kingston Rovers before it was taken for private housing. Ings Primary School and the adjacent field are on the site of another brick works and two more were incorporated into the excavation of East Park Boating Lake. Only the Willows pond remains.

When Holderness Road was still open fields with windmills here and there, and few houses except along by Thomas Street to Field Street, Witham was built up with tight courts and alleys of small dwellings. The last sign of these, Ely Place, disappeared only this summer. At the northern side of Witham in the early years of this century, there were flourishing shops, some quite small, but others, their windows protected by an arcaded front, were large stores such as Wm Craft & Sons, drapers, and Nolan's, house furnishers, in the 1920s and then, Shaw's, house furnishers, and the Premier Clothing and Supply Co. They were run-down before the war, as fewer people lived nearby and others from further out passed by on tram or trolley-bus on their way to city-centre department stores. A 1950s building, part of it even now retaining the address, 1-5 Holderness Arcade, at first the Corporation's Central Purchasing Dept., now the Supply and Printing Services, with the Environmental Health and Licensing Dept. next door at nos. 6-10 Witham, replaced the remnants of these shops after war damage. Nearer to Cleveland Street, old buildings remained. Leggett's Stores (hardware in 1921, but degenerated in time to a 'tagareen' shop) was taken by the North Eastern Trading Company, seen in this 1969 picture. Set back behind the monumental mason's yard were three-storey dwellings with balconies overhanging the drain. Inhabited up to the 1939-45 war (at least), they were relics of the early 19th century when disease was rife. Another nearby relic is the tram- or trolley-wire

connection still, in 1991, on the wall of the derelict Holderness New Inn, 28 years after the last trolley-bus on Holderness Road.

The size of the bricks of this old archway on the south side of Witham, adjoining the premises of the Discount Baby Equipment at Malton Street corner, shows that it is much earlier than nearby buildings. About 1780 it gave access to the cellar of the Bull and Dog, a public house that was renamed the Shepherd about 1830. The name fluctuated from male to female for some time, being the Shepherdess in 1835 and the Shepherd again in 1848. In 1870 it was bought by Samuel L. Doyle, a former Petty Officer on H.M.S. *Audacious*, so the inn was given the name of his ship, 'Audacious', and was sometimes known as 'The Brig Audacious'. The pub closed in 1904, but the arch survives, bricked up at the back and protected by an iron grille.

(Photo: 1968)

At the back of Holderness Road Primitive Methodist Chapel, Bright Terrace, the first on the left down Bright Street, could not have been a bright place to live. Overshadowed on its southern side by the huge chapel, near enough to the smells and smoke of Hull's riverside factories and perilously close to some of the worst disasters of the Blitz, it nevertheless survived, inhabited, into the 1960s. By then the Chapel and other buildings had gone and the terrace was open to the main road and the sunshine. From a historical point of view, we see here a Victorian terrace built in the style of many a row of Holderness cottages, with sash windows and pantiled roofs. Let not the picturesqueness of their style beguile you. For every 'little palace' in a terrace of this kind, there was a lifetime of hard graft to keep it and its occupants clean — without a bathroom and in some cases with an outside privy. This terrace was close to East Hull Baths, but who knows if some of the tenants here could afford such a luxury?

Some of the buildings, formerly houses, along Holderness Road, from Thomas Street to the Library, are among the oldest town houses in East Hull, having comprised Somerstown of the 1820s and East Parade of

(Picture taken: 1968)

a few years later. Together with Wilton Terrace at the other side of the road, they must have formed in the 1850s and after, a sort of suburbia where men rising on the ladder of commercial success chose to live. Isaac Reckitt lived in Williamson Street, Thomas Morrill in Wilton Terrace and William Field, tea dealer, at the corner of what became known as Field Street. Up to 1939 the buildings suffered changes of fortune; all on the main road were converted to shops and those in the side streets became less desirable residences than they once were. Forget their inside arrangements for a moment (they would have been built with earth closets which had to be emptied by night soil men coming through the houses) and look at the nice proportions of these grey-brick houses in Thomas Street, faint relics of the classicism of the Georgian period on the facades — and the pitted marks of shrapnel and flying debris from the Blitz.

Pemberton Street, off Dansom Lane and joining with Holborn Street, was already laid out with a couple of blocks of houses built on its northern side, when Moreland's map was published in 1834. On Goodwill and Lawson's map of 1848 it is an established street and this fine villa of the then fashionable Italianate style, shallow-roofed and with classical dignity, is shown with gardens behind it. In this 1968 picture nearly all the sash windows have been replaced, with the exception of a ground floor one at the side, still with small window panes. The houses beyond are later, probably from the 1860s. This villa was one of few of its kind and era in East Hull — or in Hull as a whole for that matter — and I was sorry when Eltherington's replaced it with modern premises. But then, it was built as a house when Pemberton Street was on the outskirts. Few people nowadays would be prepared to renovate it to the style to which it had no doubt been accustomed, add modern amenities and live in that part of town.

A great area of Studley Street had been flattened by the land mine which claimed so many lives in Ellis's Terrace, but the nearby streets, filled with crowded terraces, continued to be inhabited long after the war. The War Damage Commission replaced windows and patched up roofs etc., but the district from Dansom Lane to the railway on Holderness Road, contained many houses, substandard even in 1939. I took pictures

of John's Terrace, Charlie's Avenue etc. in Kent Street on a dull day in December 1968, when the houses were partly demolished, a pathetic sight: two up and two down, their only relief the grotesque heads over windows and doors. Nevertheless they had provided in their very closeness, a kind of security which was lacking in the promise of new houses with bathrooms and gardens on the peripheral estates. The insecurity of not knowing if old neighbours and close relatives would be able to live nearby on the estate was uppermost in many of these tenants' minds at the time.

The large-scale demolition of the 1960s revealed all kinds of oddity when buildings were open more to public view. These houses in Wilde Street, for example, had plasterwork facades. Was it a genuine attempt to make them a little different from the rest, or merely to cover shoddy brickwork? The large window is in a shop converted into a house. It had been Wheatcroft's, drapers, with all the old fitments, cubby-holes for small goods and little drawers for bobbins of cotton. The same change took place in many small shops in the side streets in the 1950s and '60s; lace curtains covered the large windows, the counters were removed and the place became a room, in some cases a reversal to its original use, as larger stores took over from the corner shops.

Wilde Street.

Poplar Buildings.

The shops between Woodhouse and Wyke Streets on Hedon Road were built in two phases in the 1880s. The roof line shows the difference in build. Those further from the camera in this picture, Alexandra Buildings, date from the time when Alexandra Dock was opened, 1885; the nearer ones up to Wyke Street are earlier. This type of dwelling did not merely provide a family home above a family shop; census retúrns show that in many cases three-storey buildings were divided into multiple occupancies. East Hull escaped the worst of this high-density building. Although there are examples on other main roads, especially Hessle Road, monotonous canyons made by long rows of three and four-storey tenements on each side of the road were, fortunately, not constructed in Hull. On Holderness Road this type of dwelling-cum-shop can be seen near Brazil Street and also near Nornabell Street. The latter block, named Poplar Buildings, has decoration in the brickwork, a fashion of the 1880s, making a band across the facade at first floor level. Similar decoration is in vogue at the moment and inset blocks of ornamental brickwork are being used on some contemporary houses, on the recent Wimpey estate north of Howdale Road, for example. Taken from beneath the overhead bridge, the picture of Poplar Buildings shows another feature, all too common after the war, but becoming rarer as old property is replaced and that is the plastered end wall, the outline of fireplace and chimney revealing that this was not the original end, but a patching up after one of the block was bombed.

Holderness Road runs across an old area of common land, the Summergangs Common, a tract of land taken up by various landowners after the 18th century Enclosures. Much of the land east of the road, that is, where Jesmond Gardens, Morrill Street, Sherburn Street, etc., etc., are now, was acquired by the Broadley family. The plots went back from Holderness Road as far as a stream running pretty well North-South from Southcoates Lane, the water wide enough

for a boat in the summer and for skating in a hard winter. At the other side of the stream was the West Field; west of Marfleet, I suppose is how the name came to be. New Bridge Road almost, but not exactly, follows this boundary ditch, a narrower road parallel to Holderness Road itself. It developed into a long shopping street after its construction in the 1890s, as more long streets were built to the east of it, bearing names of Boer War origin, Rensburg, Steynburg, etc., and with small avenues off them, some of the houses replacing dwellings demolished to make way for Alfred Gelder Street. With such an increase in housing, New Bridge Road's shops became very important as it's a long way to and from the 'Boer War' streets and Holderness Road with a full shopping basket. Nowadays New Bridge Road has many useful shops, but patterns of life have altered and more shopping is done by car. The railway bridge is still there, now carrying the high level railway line to King George Dock, but the bridge taking Craven Street over the Withernsea and goods lines is gone as there is no railway to cross. The bridge with its curious turn from Craven Street to New Bridge Road was a favourite among driving instructors in this district where slopes, let alone hills, are rare.

The delightful name of these houses on New Bridge Road derives from an early 19th-century farm of about 40 acres: Sweet Dews Farm. It was mostly grass, although there were about 12 acres of tillage in the Crowle Street area. The pebble-dashed house, with a nice garden in front, had four bedrooms, two sittingrooms, a kitchen and a dairy. Farm buildings adjacent to the house included a cow-house for 8-10 animals and, across the fold yard, stables, pigstyes, a barn and granary. The house had an open view to the River Humber. It was occupied in the middle and latter part of last century by the Pearson family, who delivered milk in the district. The grass fields also provided agistment for perhaps 30 or 40 horses while waiting to be shipped to the Continent. Modern Corporation houses now cover the area, but the name is still used: Sweet Dews Grove.

The large confident buildings of multi-departmental food stores belonging to Wm. Jackson & Son Ltd. were the result of the chairmanship and management of George Jackson Bentham, son of William Jackson of Hull. Bentham was born in 1863 and entered his father's business at the age of fifteen. He became an

active Liberal as a councillor in Hull and then, from 1910, as M.P. for Gainsborough. A comment in 1914 summed up his business acumen in describing the firm of Wm. Jackson & Son Ltd. as 'a business which has grown enormously under his guidance'. The elaborate building is on Holderness Road at the corner of Southcoates Avenue and the other, less elaborate, but with Wm. J still discernible in the upper brickwork, at the corner of Severn Street. There was another, earlier, group of shops at the corner of Bright Street. In hindsight, the development of the Supermarket with all departments under one roof, is the logical outcome of a small parade of separate shops, but it was a change that did not happen until well after the last war. Grandways, opposite Summergangs Road, is the natural descendant of Jackson's rows of shops. ASDA on the city boundary, Leo's on the former Craven Park rugby ground and Presto near Balfour Street provide competition in this type of shopping in East Hull, but 'Jackson's' is now much more than just a provision chain, having extended into other fields, wider than G. J. Bentham could have foreseen.

Commercial break.

Five advertisements from Holderness Road shops:

Wallis's shop still exists, but after a few recent years as McLeish's it is now the Newland Bakery. It was one of the many pork butcher's selling pork in season (when there was an R in the month) and cured pig products, bacon, ham, in the summer. A bakery for pork pies and sausage rolls was the usual adjunct to these shops and most of them sold sweet stuff as well. With fridges and freezers in shops and homes, people now eat pork, if they want to, at any time of the year and the description 'pork butcher' is now barely valid. Shops advertising in this way usually sell pork products, cooked meats of all kinds, sometimes dairy products, and are allied to the bread and bakery trade.

Darling's Nursery was a long greenhouse spanning the Holderness Road frontage from about No. 362 to 380, opposite Holderness House Lodge. I didn't get a picture of it, because, hearing of its imminent demolition, I went up the road one wet wintry Saturday afternoon in the late 1970s (I think) and found a merry little fire burning a pile of woodwork and everything else had been cleared away. I hope somebody recorded it as a going concern, as it was the last manifestation of an important feature of East Hull, market gardening. Beadle's on Southcoates Lane, Tattersall's on Holderness Road, where there has ever been a gap near the United Reform Church, were others in the same

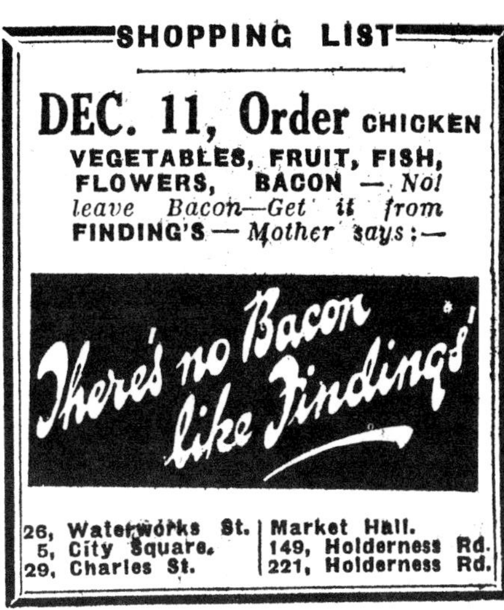

RING UP

H. P. DARLING

Holderness Road Nursery,

FOR THE—

Best Floral Work.

BOUQUETS, WREATHS & DECORATIONS AT REASONABLE CHARGES.

COR. TEL. 2045.

BACON PRICES Down Again

	per lb
• DANISH ROLL In Rashers Our own Lean Selection of Premium Brands.	1/2
• ROLLED BACON In Rashers This is a splendid Breakfast Bacon.	1/1
• MILD BACON In Rashers Cut from Selected Middles.	11d.

Get it at

CUSSONS

W. ROBINSON & SON

Ladies' & Gentlemen's

TAILOR,

223, Holderness Road,

HULL.

When requiring a NEW SUIT or LADIES' COSTUME, give us a trial.

SPECIALITY:

Robinson's Indigo Blue Serge Suits and Costumes.

OUR USUAL QUALITY.

Established 1884. Tel. 2448 Central.

Telephone: Cent. 33455.

W. M. WALLIS

Specialises in home-fed BACON AND HAMS

Pork Butcher

Finest Sausages and all kinds of Pork Products.

382 Holderness Road

1936 Prices.

line of business. Darling's greenhouse suffered during the air raids, of course, and never seemed to regain its high class image as by then the produce was not from a nearby garden. However, the flowers and plants that occupied one end of the greenhouse were always a delight to see.

Robinson's, tailors. Specialist shops were the norm rather than the exception and in the case of the tailoring trade the craftsman had his shop and workshop together. Berks was another East Hull tailor with a workshop behind Harry Abba's photographic studio at the top of Williamson Street. Clearly these men knew their trade; in Robinson's case it was carried on by his son, Peter, in a shop opposite East Park until quite recent times. But there were retail specialists, too, where the assistants knew what they were selling, be it drapery or grocery, greengrocery or ironmongery. Nowadays the true specialists are rarer as more goods are pre-packaged and sold by assistants with less knowledge of the products than used to be the case.

Finding's. Chain stores were set up between the wars and there were the Maypoles, Liptons, Gallons etc. all over the place. Even so, people made their choice, preferring one shop's butter to another, and a third shop's cheese. Labelled packages, covering products that are virtually the same, were not so prevalent as now, especially for perishable goods. Competition was strong between many of these shops and they advertised frequently to keep their names in the public mind. Here is a slightly less well-known firm, Finding's, advertising at the time of the abdication of Edward VIII, December, 1936. The prices are interesting at Cusson's, the same date.

Opened on the day of Queen Victoria's Golden Jubilee 21 June, 1887, East Park was to provide a recreational space at the edge of East Hull, at that time accessible by horse tramcar. The first park occupied the area between what became Summergangs Road to East Park Avenue, with its far boundary along the Lambwath Stream, which until 1929, was Hull's boundary also. East Park was laid out with gardens, lakes and artificial hills created for variety. A winding lake opened into two ponds and this bridge spanned the entrance to one of them. This postcard was used in 1906 and so the view could be some time before that. Between the two ponds a bandstand, was a popular attraction on Sunday afternoons, when the East Hull Prize Silver Band was performing from 3 till 5 o'clock. The programmes were quite wide-ranging in appeal, of sacred and secular pieces, individuals showing their musical skill in solos. For example, on 19 August 1906 the Hull Royal Infirmary East Hull Working Men's Committee arranged the concert and the band played:

March, Punchinello;
Overture, Caliph of Bagdad;
Selection, Polinto;
Cor Solo, The Chorister; Interval
Air Varie, Vesper Hymn;
Grand Selection, Souvenir de Meyerbeer;
Euphonium Solo, Nazareth;
Chorus, Hallelujah.

As always, the band, at that time conducted by J. G. Longman, ended with God Save the King.

Connecting two of the artificial hills in East Park was this bridge over an equally artificial gorge, dubbed Khyber Pass. After the Wembley Exhibition of 1928, the carved wooden doors from the African Pavilion were erected in the arch under the bridge. They had been copied from an Arab doorway in Zanzibar and this spot in the park had an air of mystery, not Eastern mystery because of its connections but rather dismal mystery as it was somewhat sunless and damp and there were 'dungeons' set into the wall of the gorge. A real mystery of East Park, however, concerns two ancient stone arches from Newark Castle, first re-erected in the

grounds of Holderness House and then given by Mrs. Jalland about 1900 to the Parks Committee. The stones were numbered, the arches dismantled and dumped near the park greenhouses among a lot of pavers etc. and also old stonework from Suffolk Palace in Lowgate (the house of the de la Poles, acquired by Henry VIII in 1539, where the General Post Office now stands). The City Engineer of 1922, when questioned, said he did not know that there had been any historical significance attached to the stones; the feeling had been that in the improbable event of there being any money to spare, the Parks Committee had more pressing calls for it. Sic transit...

In 1913, Mr. T. R. Ferens presented a tract of land for a boating lake, thereby increasing the park to its present size. Sparse trees in the early days allow us to see that James Reckitt Avenue was not yet built. On the land beyond the island, I can just discern a windpump, probably a relic from the brickworks that existed here. At the back of the picture to the right is a double fronted house at the correct angle to be Sutton House, but it seems too close. Maps of the time show Sutton House and Ings House Farm as the only buildings which could possibly be visible, but the farm, being on Ings Road opposite the present opening to James Reckitt Avenue, is hardly likely, so what is seen must be Robson's Sutton House at the top of Ings Road. All the area behind the park was, until 1929, in the East Riding, the edge of the park being the town boundary till then. James Reckitt and the Avenues round about, all private housing, were built up in the inter-war period and Ings Estate constructed for the Corporation in the 1960s, so that now East Park is more centrally situated for the population it usually serves.

In the minutes of the Parks and Burials Committee for 12 February 1930, the Park Superintendent's Report announced the following plan for East Park. '...during the coming summer I hope to make a show of antirrhinums around the Watch Tower which was taken from the old Town Hall.' However, the Town Hall relic is in Pearson Park and the plaque beneath the only watch tower that I have known in East Park declares itself thus: 'This watch tower is the only relic of the old Hull citadel commonly called "The Garrison" which was situated at the junction of the rivers Humber and Hull on the east bank of the latter river. The barbican-like turret was the most advanced work of the western bastion and surmounted the apex of the angle of the south and west glacis of the fortress. The citadel was dismantled by the Crown in 1863-4. Part of its site afterwards became the property of the late Mr. Wm. Bailey, Esq. J.P., of Hull and Winestead Hall ... steamship owner and director of the Hull Dock Co. The watch tower had then been built into the walls of the Humber Iron Works ship-building yard owned by Mr. Bailey....' The tower was presented to the city in 1912 by Mr. Bailey's family and trustees. In my recollection the plaque has always been accessible to be read from the path without flower beds underneath it. The hilly parts where the tower is sited have been known as Spion Kop and round the corner, near the entrance to Khyber Pass, was an old First World War tank, I have been told. Citadel tower, Khyber Pass, Spion Kop, dungeons, old tank — what a collection of warlike memorabilia for a peaceful place! Nowadays the graffiti writers are the enemy, leaving their mark even on the tower itself.

Before major State intervention in education by the Forster Act of 1870, the churches established many schools, offering an elementary curriculum, different from the older Grammar Schools. Two organisations, the National Society for the Propagation of Christian Knowledge, the N.S.P.C.K., and the British and Foreign Schools Society, the B.F.S.S., were also active in promoting elementary education, the former supported by Anglicans, the British Society by Non-conformists. There were many Non-conformists and a strong Quaker influence in East Hull even in its early days before the large Methodist chapels were built. Consequently, a British School was established in Dansom Lane in 1838. It flourished, being regarded as one of the town's best schools and members of the Reckitt family were prominent in its management. Holderness Ward British School closed when the Hull School Board was set up after the Education Act, but it had to be re-opened for a while to provide space for the greater number of children attending, as Williamson Street Board School was not yet built. The British School building was later used by the firm of T. T. Cass, cabinetmakers, and this name is still there in the marble step at the front. More recently the facade has

been altered and painted so that the date is obliterated and the character of the original lost. This picture was taken in 1970.

The Roman Catholic school, St. Mary's in Wilton Street, served also as a mission hall from its opening in 1856 until until the church was built next to it in 1891. The only Catholic school in East Hull before the 1870 Act, it was staffed by the Sisters of Mercy until after World War Two, by which time the school was partly the responsibility of the Local Education Committee. St. Mary's continued well into the 1960s, and this photo was taken in 1970 when I was collecting pictures of schools for the centenary of the first Education Act.

This is 'Chappie', Chapman Street School, built 1885, demolished 1991. To plot the positions and check the dates of schools is a rough-and-ready way of finding out the changes of population of an area. Pre-State schools, that is, pre-1870 schools, in East Hull were in Prospect Place, Drypool; St. Mark Street; Dansom Lane; Wilton Street and Southcoates. By 1870 industry and population were well on the increase east of the river. The Hull School Board becamed active in the early 1870s: Courtney Street and Lincoln Street, the town's second and third Board Schools respectively, Williamson Street 1875, Stoneferry Road 1877, Lime Street 1879 and Buckingham Street 1882. Courtney Street School went with the homes it served during the clearance of the early 1970s; about that time, I took a picture of a grandmother, mother and two boys standing outside the closed school. All had attended it and perhaps great-grandmother also, but in 1970 they were apprehensively awaiting the move to Bransholme.

Chapman Street's numbers were falling before the war and after the Junior Dept. was bombed in 1941, a mixed, all-age school continued in the rest of the building until Hull's first comprehensive, David Lister, opened in 1964.

The cupola from the roof of Chapman Street School has been modified and now stands as a clock tower outside Broady's demolition yard on Stoneferry Road. Comparison with the original shows that most of the louvres have been removed and the clock added, a smart and useful piece of renovation.

Malet Lambert High School opened in 1932 as successor to the over-crowded Craven Street Higher Grade School. The new school was planned in an E-shape, providing central administration, assembly hall and gymnasium block, with workshops, domestic science rooms and laboratories on the outer arms of the E. Classrooms arranged along the front of the building allowed for partial separation of the sexes in this mixed school, as boys' classes and facilities were at the caretaker's lodge side and the girls' at the other end. At first, there were single-sex classes until the 5th (School Certificate) year, but the exigencies of evacuation and staff call-up changed that. The building escaped major damage, but a stick of small H.E.s made craters across the Gillshill Road field, an inconvenience put right by every games class walking in line across the field and collecting lumps of clay in paper carriers. Senior boys rolled the surface level after the earth had been thrown back into the bomb-holes. Additional facilities have been provided in more recent years on the edge of the field at the back of the school, at first to account for the wider range of ability when the school became comprehensive, other classrooms for music etc. and a sports complex away from the main building. Now the school caters for pupils aged from eleven to sixteen across the ability range. The sixth form honours board at the back of the hall records the academic success of some well-known Old Students including Jean Rook, with pride of place given to the memorial to 2nd Lt. John Harrison, V.C., M.C. The citation describes his 'most conspicuous bravery and self-sacrifice' in leading a company of men against an enemy machine-gun post in darkness and thick gun-smoke. After two unsuccessful sorties, Harrison made a single-handed dash at the machine-gun post, an action which cost his life at the age of 26. He had been a pupil at Craven Street from 1901 to 1909.

The very young ladies of Hornsea House private school pose for a photograph in 1921. The school was in one of the villas of Hornsea Parade, grey brick and quite large enough for the purpose, according to the standards of the time. One such villa remains, now transformed into the Craven Park public house. Hornsea House was behind it with its frontage facing south, that is, at right angles to the main road. As seen here, there was a grass plot and shrubs, for use as a playground. It was a girls' school, but from something I was told, I have the impression that a few small boys may have also been admitted. The proprietors were Charles and Mary Rowell, with Mrs. Rowell running the school, and their daughters, Maggie, Dorothy and Florence acting as teachers. In the 1921 Directory, a Miss Brown, teacher, was recorded as being at Hornsea House, so she must have been another member of staff. It was one of a few private schools on Holderness Road, along with the Misses Keers' at Studley House and Madame Hall's at The Willows.

Photo: courtesy of Mr. R. E. Kims

Thomas Robinson Ferens (1847-1930) was so well known as to be referred to as Tommy Ferens or T.R.F., in a familiar but not disrespectful way by many people. He came to Hull from County Durham as a

young man, and rose from his first position as confidential clerk at Reckitt's to become Director of the company. Unlike some others of his time and later, who moved out of East Hull, usually west to Pearson Park, Newland Park or Hessle, when they reached a certain level of success, Ferens stayed East. In 1874 he was living at 1, Filey Parade, Holderness Road at the corner of Buckingham Street before the school was built; he then moved to Saxby House (now Pramland) in 1889 and stayed there until 1905. His next home was Wilton House, where the old people's home now is, and, finally, from 1910, Holderness House until his death. Here Mr. and Mrs. Ferens pose on the steps of Holderness House, the date, I judge, being in the early 1920s.

I was privileged to be allowed by Mr. and Mrs. M. J. Fenton, the present owners of Saxby House, now Pramland, a shop selling a wide range of nursery equipment, to go through the deeds. This enabled me to find out that the land from Southcoates Lane to near Jesmond Gardens and as far back as New Bridge Road had, in 1814, belonged to the Rev. Thomas Broadley, a bachelor, who left it to his brother Henry. It apparently passed to William Henry Harrison, who

annexed the name Broadley at the wish of his aunt, Sophia Broadley. Ald. Robert Waller bought a strip of this land in 1876 and at his death in 1888, a contract to sell to Mr. Ferens had already been drawn up. The deeds do not show when Saxby House was built, but it was before 1886 and I think therefore that Robert Waller must have bought the plot on which to build.

Garden Village in its early days before the First World War: well-built houses with modern amenities, even bathrooms in some cases. They have stood the test of time and, after a period when East Hull was distinctly unfashionable, have come into their own again as desirable residences close enough to the city centre, not polluted by the smells and smoke of factories. In this picture, Beech Avenue leads off bottom left, with Village Road (that was originally Chestnut Crescent) to the right. Beyond are Elm Avenue leading to The Oval and Maple Grove. The mature elm trees in this picture have gone, but in the 80-odd years since the roadside saplings were planted, their growth has completely transformed the scene.

Picture courtesy of Mr. J. W. Houlton

Tucked in between Portobello Street and The Broadway is a small village, built for employees of the British Oil and Cake Mills after the First World War. Although much smaller, it is of the style of Reckitt's Garden Village. BOCM Village was opened on 23 July, 1921, when 56 houses of the projected 112 first phase were already built. The total plan was never completed but the houses were interestingly designed and well constructed. Rents originally were from 10/6 (52½p) to 15/- (75p) per week, showing decisively that the houses were not intended for the lowest-paid workers. During World War I, BOCM had developed New Pin Soap, a hard soap for household cleaning and after the war this became so successful a line that Seafield Avenue in the Village was almost named after it. As in the Garden Village, the roadside trees are now very large, their roots crack the pavements and their foliage is so dense as to create an almost dismal shade. The houses, though, are back in vogue; with their timbered gables they have the appearance of some 1990s 'executive' houses.

Newtown Buildings, built on 'Nanny Goat Field' in 1931-2, were part of an inter-war re-housing scheme. In one of the worst positions imaginable during the war, they became, in the post-war period, run down and hardly desirable residences. 1984 was the year in which they became Hull's first 'priority estate' and in 1986 they underwent an improvement scheme costing £100,000. The scheme involved providing security of windows, doors, stairs and landings and an entry 'phone system. It was associated with the opening of a new Council office and a laundrette, the aim being not merely to deal with the fabric, but to re-form a community by involving the tenants in the planning and implementation of improvements. In liaison with the Doorstep Trust, 26 shared flatlets were provided in the summer of 1987 to help meet the needs of young single people. Now called Newtown Court, the flats, seen through a leafy screen on the dockside, present an almost unrecognisable picture in comparison with a few years ago.

Three Housing Acts had great influence on the inter-war build-up of towns. The Addison Act of July, 1919, gave impetus to the building of Council houses, as Local Authorities were able to add one penny (1d) to the rates for that purpose and the Treasury would pay the remainder. The Chamberlain Act (1923) encouraged private building by direct subsidy, a system which continued up to the Second World War. Wheatley's Act of 1924, emanating from the Labour

government, was directed towards the construction of rented Council housing, but without rescinding the subsidy on private building. The names of Addison, Chamberlain and Wheatley Gardens in Summergangs Road are reminders of these Acts. Hull Corporation housing really started with the Addison Act. East Hull Estate was one of the first major projects, its initial phase being from December, 1921, with 200 houses completed by January, 1923. At the following weekly rents:

13/6	(67½p)	parlour, 3-bed.
12/-	(60p)	non-parlour, 3-bed.
10/-	(50p)	non-parlour, 2-bed.

with additional rates and water charges, many new tenants, especially those in the 'parlour' type, found it difficult to make ends meet and moved away. However, a report of 1927 showed a clear demand for the smaller houses. By the time the 1930 Ordnance Survey map was published, East Hull Estate was much as we know it today. It catered at first for people who had lived in slums elsewhere, was commonly called Corn Beef Island, and stories of coals in the bath were bandied about (by people who didn't live there). Of course there were those who did not make the best of the new situation, but the vast majority revelled in lighter houses with amenities and gardens and the possibility of allotment gardens in addition. Housing and other authorities over the years have had the recurring or even constant task of trying to overcome the problems which beset certain areas. Renovation and demolition of some houses have improved the outward appearance of parts of the estate, but still there are gardens filled with household débris or merely left to rough grass. The renovated houses have the in-vogue appearance with little pointed porch roofs etc., but here in Kilnsea Grove and Portobello Street are the unadorned, archetypal 1920s Council houses.

Sutton Trust Estate is coincidentally not far from the parish of Sutton, but the name Sutton here is that of William Richard Sutton, who, after a lifetime in the carrier business left accumulated wealth of over £2 million in 1900, most of which was to be used in setting up a charitable trust for the provision of model, low-rent dewellings for the poor of London 'and other populous places'. Hull's turn to benefit from this came in 1930 when a 40-acre site was bought for £4,800. The 476 houses and 24 flats completed in 1932 cost about £218,000. For comparison, in-filling schemes completed in 1964 adding 13 bungalows and 12 flats cost £55,000 and another 5 bungalows in 1981, about £95,000. Rents in 1932 were 4/6 per week (22½p). This is Shelley Avenue, not in memory of the poet, but

as with many in Sutton Trust, the name of one of the trustees. Others include Watson, Wakefield, Fremantle, Forber, Kyffin-Taylor, Carden and Collin. The last-named was James Barnes Collin who became Managing Director and then Chairman of Sutton & Co., Carriers.

Snugly surrounded by hedges and shrubs of more than forty years' growth, this is one of the prefabs that were an emergency housing measure after the war. They were erected in clusters or little estates all over Hull soon after the cessation of hostilities in 1945 and were well-planned to provide compact living

Maybury Road.

Bellfield Avenue.

accommodation. They had drawbacks of cold in winter, overheating in summer and condensation when there was a change in the weather, but very many people were better housed in them than they would have been in the old Victorian terraces. Despite their faults, the prefabs were reckoned to be so successful that one from Yardley, Birmingham, of the Arcon Mark V type made by Taylor-Woodrow, has been re-erected and furnished according to late 1940s standards at the National Museum of Building, Avoncroft, near Bromsgrove. In East Hull, those on Holderness High Road were pulled down in the 1970s. Hopewell Road's prefabs and also those in the Broadway have gone. The Gillshill Road site was cleared in July, 1991, and perhaps the rest of these in Maybury Road will have undergone the same fate by now. Emergency measure or no, they outlasted some other post-war housing by many years, while another type of prefabrication, the Spooner houses in Bellfield Avenue appear to be still 'going strong'.

Longhill Estate, the district enclosed by Holderness High Road, Ganstead Lane, Holderness Drain and Saltshouse Road had the natural advantage of some mature trees in the middle of it and at least one major boundary that was not a straight line. Thus, the main thoroughfare, Shannon Road, curves gently and at the point where a shopping parade was provided, the trees

add some grace to the scene. Longhill followed the post-war baby boom by a few years so that in 1957 the primary school's admissions class had 81 children in it, if reports of the time were true. Certainly it started as a district full of young children, for many of whom, now adults, the memory of open countryside so near to their homes must be an important feature of their childhood.

These houses will no doubt benefit from part of the £26 million renovation programme announced on 4 June 1991 by the city's Housing Chairman, Cllr. John Black. Abutting the earlier Sutton Trust Estate they

are in the pre-war section of Bilton Grange, built to re-house people from Victorian housing in the streets and terraces off Hedon Road and elsewhere. The project was interrupted by the 1939-45 war, after which the need was even more urgent, as many people were living in multiple occupancy of old, damaged houses and the air-raids had savagely done the work of slum-clearance.

Even in the flat, featureless Bilton Grange, where a truly mature tree is a rarity and facades are remarkably similar from road to road there are more gracious areas and well-kept gardens. Here, on Milne Road, the open green has rapidly-growing trees and a mixture of houses and bungalows precludes the uniformity occurring on some other estate roads. This is in the post-war section of Bilton Grange. Many roads were

laid before the war as the need for better housing was already all too evident. The estate took its name from the 313 acre Bilton Grange Farm, its buildings being about the place where Barham Road bends near the primary school. To the east of the school, in the Parthian, Griffin, Amethyst Road district was Bilton Low Bottoms, a name telling us something about the state of the land before proper drainage was undertaken.

Ings Estate has characteristics not found in any other East Hull estate, because it is situated on the slope up to the ridge that forms Sutton village and part of Saltshouse Road. The arrangement of the houses is different from the other estates, too, as there are small squares around grass plots that are inward-looking like the old street terraces, but with far more space. These two features together, the arrangement and the gradients, make parts of the estate confusing to a newcomer or to someone trying to find a short cut. There are the sloped underpasses, of course, but also narrow ways with steps that are unique. Camberwell Way is a footpath about on the line of the old Bellfield Avenue beyond the Lambwath Stream. Petersham Close is near the site of Bellfield (or Bellefield) House, once the home of Benjamin Pickering, and some of its old trees remain. A belt of trees down Bellfield and up to the house on Saltshouse Road (it was directly opposite the entrance to Sutton Annexe, now the Princess Royal Hospital), formed a screen for the lawns and meadow at the south side of the house. This woodland was a happy hunting-ground for children until its demolition in 1965, especially after the war when the house stood empty for a long time, although the lodges were still occupied. The trees were a deciduous mixture, with some yew and holly, the ground covered with ivy and lesser periwinkle. In spring there were snowdrops, violets, cuckoo pint and an occasional primrose. I have seen pheasants here and partridges were nesting in the meadow where Mitcham Road had been constructed in the 1960s just before houses were built. Open spaces have been left, and some of the original hedgerows, too, especially behind the Grasby Road area up to the newer stretch of Bellfield Avenue. On Ings Road beyond the houses pictured here, are a few trees, including some oaks, which I hope will be preserved even if the field they border has eventually to be built upon.

Greatfield Estate is a deceptive place. Less than a mile from end to end, it nevertheless seems much larger. It always feels remote to me and I suppose that is due to the long stretch of open road past the Eastern Cemetery, before the estate is reached. Greatfield roughly parallels the city's eastern boundary, finishing a good way from Hedon Road, where an area has developed as an industrial estate. Annandale Road, Greatfield's main artery, continues Preston Road to the east, then sweeps round to come into Grange Road at the Wingfield Road junction. Greatfield's schools, churches, few shops and nice houses do not seem to redeem this estate from a cold flatness, as though every wind from Siberia had swept over the Plain of

Ecclesfield Avenue.

Holdeness and levelled Greatfield even before the post-war planners set to work. Ecclesfield Avenue, about opposite Kingston Rovers' new Craven Park, is the most westerly of the estate and these houses share with others on Greatfield a view of the cranes and funnels of King George Dock.

Bransholme took its name from two farms that were there when Smeaton surveyed the open drains in the 18th century, High Bransholme and Low Bransholme, the names an indication that the land was not absolutely flat. Very slight knolls here and there gave drier ground for farm buildings, the old 'holmr' meaning a hillock in watery surroundings. There is a slight rise up to Wawne Road through Littleham Close and I was amazed to see that, with all the perfectly flat land round about, a group of old persons' bungalows had been built exactly on the edge of the rise, so there is a considerable gradient for older or handicapped persons up to the front doors. That noticed, I realised that Lambwath Hall was built on higher ground, too. Trees of part of its estate remain at the junction of Wawne Road and Biggin Avenue. Housing on Bransholme has a wide green belt up to the city boundary and open countryside beyond, except for the furthest stretch of Cumbrian Way that is parallel to the northern boundary, and has fields only a few yards away. Much of Bransholme is individual housing and there are several schools. The so-called 'Alcatraz' flats that were found to be so extremely unsatisfactory were pulled down, but there are a few high-rise blocks of a different build. The main roads may be crossed by underpasses although as I have walked about this and other estates, I have noticed that many people prefer to cross on the surface. Car owners have been catered for by the provision of blocks of garages. Two views show different aspects: a panorama of houses and a high-rise block off Noddle Hill Way and the trees of Wawne Road.

Here and there on Bransholme are a few shops, but the main shopping concourse is the Bransholme Centre, where the buses converge. Covered arcades of the most

commonly used type of shop have an indoor market attached, the only real difference to the shopper being in the stall-like arrangement there as distinct from the 'covered street' feel of the other malls. The centre is kept far freer of litter than the estate outside by the constant effort of sweepers and although not in the forefront of design and elegance, the shopping centre serves people as well as its size allows. There are pubs, clubs, library and a health centre attached, and, across Goodhart Road, the Methodist Church and a community centre.

Contiguous to Bransholme is Sutton Park, a private housing estate which swallowed up the site of the Evan Fraser Isolation Hospital and an amount of land around it. The estate is shielded from the hammer of ring road traffic by grass and banked gardens on Sutton Road. Built in the 1970s, about the same time as parts of Bransholme, it has a variety of house construction and a good deal more variety due to individual householder's tastes. It has several schools, including fairly late manifestations of Church provision of

education in St. Andrew's C. of E. and St. Anne's R.C. Schools, both now under the aegis of the Humberside Education Authority. On the open space between the Bransholme Centre and Sutton Park estate is the modern Catholic church of Mary, Queen and Martyr, with a belfry of five curiously-toned bells that chime the hours and the quarters. Names of thoroughfares on Sutton Park are all '-dales' without 'street', 'grove' or 'avenue'. Here is Marsdale, showing the underpass to cross Newtondale and some chestnut trees which, I believe, show it to be near the Evan Fraser hospital site.

In 1921, a pamphlet was distributed in East Hull as part of the Drypool Parish Appeal. In it Canon Berry commented on the 'congestion of population' in parts of the parish. 'In one street alone there are no fewer than 570 houses with a population of nearly 3,000. There are no tenements, no cellar-dwellings, no back-to-back houses, but in parts there is a great deal of squalor, and one saw in passing through the parish far too many ragged, unkempt and shoeless children.' Not all the old streets have been riven apart for slum clearance. Instead, in Franklin and Brazil Streets, for example, ends of terraces have been pulled down and neat communal gardens planted with grass plots and pretty shrubs. They provide quiet breathing spaces, allowing light and air into nearby houses. Beyond these streets, on the south side of Abbey Street, where there were Hollis's sawmills and woodyards and railway marshalling yards, a new generation of housing is being constructed, starting with the delightfully named Rosey Row, bungalows with little gardens, near Williamson Street School. This is urban renewal.

Off Redcar Street, too, where the air is far cleaner than when these houses were built, Laburnum Grove presents anything but an image of inner city housing, with the roses blooming.

Off Redcar Street.

After the war there was the problem, not only of re-building, but what to do with the unusable rubble from bomb-damage clearance. One solution was to build a mound, an artificial feature in this area, but welcome as a wind-break, a slide or a mere variation of view, across the otherwise rather gaunt Ald. Kneeshaw playing fields next to the high flats of Valiant Drive on Bilton Grange. Not many high rise flats were built in Hull and the city sky-scape from outside the boundary has a rather gap-toothed appearance in consequence. The view from the top of the Valiant Drive flats on a clear day is stunning, but I think it is well that the houses, the remains of which form the ridge beside the flats, were not replaced wholesale by high-rise building, desirable as it seemed to planners at the time.

Ald. Kneeshaw Playing Field.

To travel through East Hull is to ask what people do in their leisure time. There's plenty of open evidence of a fair number of gardeners, but most of the meetings of a social or cultural nature are hidden in schools or church halls with little publicity. There are very many women's meetings, with hard-working committees providing interesting programmes for members — the Townswomen's Guilds, British Legion and those associated with every denomination of church — and there are Education Committee leisure classes in the

larger schools, a University of the Third Age at the former school on Ings Road and a flourishing mixed adult choir at Malet Lambert. For the majority who want something different from these, there are plenty of pubs and clubs and two sports centres. Of these, let the Elephant and Castle represent the former as it's one of those pubs that started as a little corner shop and blossomed into its present form; and let Ennerdale, near the river on Sutton Road, larger than the other (the Woodford Centre at East Park) and of the glass and metal architecture of the 80s, be illustrative of some of East Hull's sports interests.

A modern phenomenon-with-a-difference is the appearance, in the last few years, of markets springing up in unlikely places. Where once the market came to the community and was in the centre of a town or village, of easy access to the inhabitants, the car now rules and markets are set up on the periphery of the city or right outside and the customer travels to it. Such a market is set up on Wednesdays and Saturdays on land adjoining Hull Kingston Rovers' new ground near Poorhouse Lane, on the edge of Greatfield. There is a fair range of goods on sale — drapery, rugs, plants, food etc. — with the inevitable fast snack stalls and some entertainment for children. The car park was full when I went, but there were others like myself travelling by bus and also nearer residents walking there for a different style of Saturday afternoon shopping.

Built in 1934, the Astoria is one of very few Hull cinemas that have survived in anything like their original form. Outwardly, at least, the Astoria looks just the same as it always did; only the advertisements are different: bingo instead of films. It was closed as a cinema in the 1960s and the organ, which changed colour with the lamps inside it, is now in the Museum of Mechanical Music at Rufforth, near York.

The following are possibly social history, but, to most older cinema-goers, pure nostalgia, especially the prices. Some of these cinemas were not in East Hull, as they operated in groups.

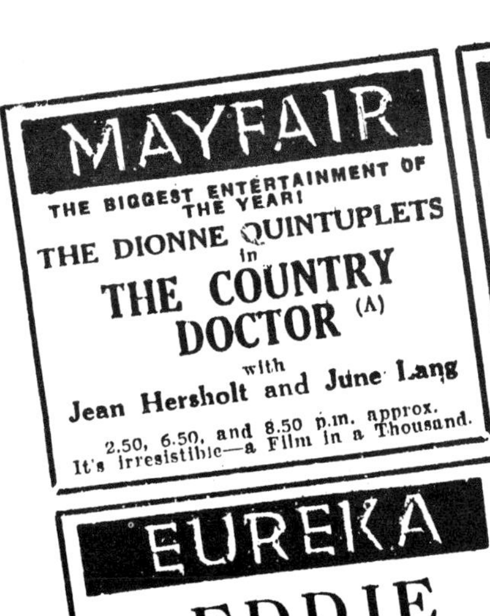

Beyond the hedge of the old Hornsea railway track on the north side towards Leads Road, is a rare stretch of countryside: Rockford Fields. In summer the ground is a thickly matted meadow of vetches, yellow rattle, clovers and 'marguerite' daisies, hung over with the song of skylarks. Meadow pipits also nest here, probably the reason why the cuckoo can be seen and heard quite regularly in the early summer, seeking nests in which to lay eggs. Adjacent to Rockford Fields is a rough tract of land, almost impenetrably covered with brambles, a haven for undisturbed wild-life.

These areas have been the subject of controversy for many years, the most recent outcry being the protests organised in the past couple of years and still being pursued. The land belongs to the Corporation, but its earlier status is a bit of a mystery, local folk-lore regarding it as common land. Some of it is fenced off now and building begun, but Rockford Fields have for the time being escaped total disaster, as planning permission has been given for only a limited number of houses on the Leads Road side. With Hull's population declining, the continued demand for houses to fill every pleasantly free area seems contradictory. With international movements towards conservation, the despoilation of Rockford Fields is as serious an issue in its way as the felling of the rain forests.

When the Hull Corporation electric tramway was brought down Holderness Road as far as Aberdeen Street, the tramsheds were built there in 1903. An unprepossessing, functional building, it nevertheless had a lively terra-cotta facade of a rich and subtle red. The design was quite original, quirky and fun. Heraldic lions were poised on pedestals at the top, there were turrets, scrolls and leaves, rounded arches and square-headed windows, a jumble, a mixture, but harmonious and above all different. Suddenly, with no public notice that I am aware of, no time for protest by

an enraged East Hull public, no outcry from the Civic Society, on 20 May 1988 demolition began and in a very short time was too far advanced to do anything about it. The idignity was that it wasn't totally demolished, but boarded up for months before the final coup de grace. What a theatrical entrance the facade would have made to Leo's new superstore! But no, now there are only old photographs and a few fragments which (I was told) somebody took home for his rockery.

The foundation stone of the original Hedon Road prison was laid 9 October 1865 by the Mayor, H. J. Atkinson. Sheahan, the historian, in describing the building, came to the regrettable conclusion that it was 'nondescript' as far as style and beauty were concerned, being of a debased pointed style known as Carpenters' Gothic. Even so, the plan, ventilation and drainage were said to be excellent. The people of Hull, however, were scandalised to find that the projected cost was £56,000. The prison's conical green tower has become a landmark and the gaol itself, originally designed for 347 prisoners in separate cells, has undergone several transformations in its internal arrangements and use. As with other old town prisons, it was on a suburban site at first, but quite rapidly became surrounded in a growing urban area. On the west side, across Southcoates Lane, is Newtown Court, and to the east the Corporation Cemetery presents a well-kept picture of rose-beds on the Hedon Road frontage, flanked by the high prison wall. A cause for concern has been the necessity of housing young people on remand in cramped conditions in the prison's B-wing. The opening of another gaol near Doncaster in August, 1991, is intended to relieve pressure on accommodation in Hull, by the removal of these remand prisoners and leave the way clear for a £1 million refurbishment of B-wing.

East Hull has been a safe Labour seat since 1945, the two Members who have served in that time, Commander Pursey and John Prescott, enjoying large majorities. It was not ever thus. Liberal representation, also with large majorities, was the norm up to 1884, when Hull was re-formed into three constituencies, each with one Member. Liberalism continued to be the prevailing force in East Hull although there were two defeats — in 1886 and 1895 — to Conservatives. By the outbreak of World War I, T. R. Ferens had represented East Hull for about 12 years under the Liberal banner, but he was defeated by a Coalition

Unionist in 1918. Between the wars, Labour candidates entered the ring, increasing their vote at each election. There were very strong Conservative elements in parts of East Hull, but Labour was increasingly considered the most viable alternative at national government level, and Liberalism had had its day as far as local representation was concerned. In 1922 L. R. Lumley, who became the Earl of Scarborough, issued this card as an election advert. and was returned again after two years in the House. By 1929, with George Muff's election, Labour had made its mark on East Hull, and, although Muff was out of office 1931-5, he was back in again in 1935, the start of Labour supremacy in all Parliamentary elections since.

Common features of all industrial city-scapes, gas-holders still have their use as storage, even though there has been no need for the dirty, smelly old gas-works that usually were beside them since piped North Sea gas replaced manufactured town gas. The gas-holder in St. Mark Street, however, is not used and viewed through the flora of the once Foredyke Stream looks like a giant open-air sculpture, a not unpleasing memorial to times past.

Not 'change and decay', but decay, then change.

The Victoria Dock slipway in October, 1984, was a sad scene to anyone who had worked there. By the spring of 1990, operations at the Citadel site and the Victoria Dock Estate were well advanced, and a few months later the slipway had become an ornamental pool among modern houses, as seen in the following three pictures.

Photos: courtesy of Mr. E. Storr

The river frontage looking towards the Humber Bridge from close by the ornamental pool on a sunny May morning (1991) gives the impression of some south coast Riviera, minus palm trees. Oh, that the tide of Humber may be contained by the new embankment, and that the houses are sufficiently insulated against the wind! But what a nice prom, prom, prom to stroll along.

At the same time as the modern steel-and-glass architecture is being used (and criticised) in large scale

projects, there is a return to a Victorian cottage style for domestic building. Here to the north of Sutton are bungalows with features not truly indigenous to Holderness — projecting windows, barge boards and finials. A cluster of these bungalows and houses reminds me of the tied dwellings of some great landed estate and the features which are charming individually become overwhelming when repeated on every one.

Founded in 1853 and operational until 1932, Earles' was at one time synonymous with shipbuilding, and the company far better remembered than any others in that line in Hull because of its longevity. Other firms, such as Martin Samuelson's and Brownlow and Pearson, had remarkable output, especially about the middle of the last century when iron ships were rapidly overtaking the number of wooden ones. For half a century ship-building was non-existent in East Hull, until the Yorkshire Dry Dock Co. started building in Lime Street and launching the vessels sideways into the river. On 21 October, 1987, the contract was placed with the firm and on 26 November that year the keel laid of a new venture, the *Ra*, a luxurious Nile cruiser, to be operated between Cairo, Luxor and Aswan. The *Ra* was launched by Mrs. Fatima Allam on 18 April, 1988, and subsequently further decks were added and fitting-out completed. In my view, the huge superstructure tends to overwhelm the elegant line of the vessel's hull, but the upper works are all part of the five-star accommodation and amenities. Here the bridge deck and sundeck steelwork is being added after the launch into the River Hull, and since then people passing regularly over North Bridge have been able to witness in the construction of an even larger craft of this type, the unfolding of one of Hull's modern success stories.

(Picture by courtesy of Mr. J. Dempster)

Here is that 'large and deep river called by the town's name': at the mouth the Tidal Barrier and Myton Bridge; the view upstream from North Bridge;

downstream from the high steps on Stoneferry Road; another downstream view from the new Stoneferry Bridge... the river that defines east and west in this city.

Is there really much difference between East and West Hull?

Well, on *that* side of the river they favoured black and white, on *this* side, red and white. At one time, Rugby supporters had to choose the nearer team, because a ticket plus a tram ride cost too much, or a long walk took too much precious spare time. Nowadays, although I dare say that the majority of Rovers' fans are from east of the river, I know it to be not an exclusively East Hull crowd; there are those who cross the river both ways. However, from its early beginnings as White Star, playing on Mr. Pearson's field at Sweet Dews Farm, Kingston Rovers has been nearly all its time an East Hull club. What has changed, apart from the grounds, from Craven Street to Craven Park to Poorhouse Lane, are the spectators. Look at this flat-capped crowd in the threepenny (3d) stand at the back of the tramsheds in April, 1925, a match against Wigan: three women only, no favours, just a crowd of fellows *determined* to have a good afternoon. Compare it with a match today.

Photo: courtesy the Secretary, Hull Kingston Rovers.

Touring East Hull and looking at it in detail has been, on the whole, a heartening experience. It is no Utopia, nor is it more the Christian side of the city than the west is, but the general level of housing is much higher than in my childhood days.

Smells of the seed-crushing industry have almost gone. An occasional rancid odour when the wind has changed to a westerly can precede rain like the smell of fish used to do, and a summertime whiff of Saltend's chemicals often heralds a south-easterly breeze to keep Hull cool and cloudy while further inland enjoys a heatwave. Some of the old sounds have diminished, too. 'Foggy early on', 'Aye, I 'eard fog'orns', is a common enough exchange on an autumn morning, and, as much of the docking facility for larger ships is now east of the River Hull, the foghorns' mournful cries may now be an East Hull singularity. Certainly the old custom of bringing in the New Year with a fanfare of ships' hooters was not a prerogative of the east side. In recent years the custom has dwindled with the number of ships in dock to more of a melancholy Last Post to the old year than the former joyful cacophony of welcome to the new. Perhaps this will change as trade picks up. One regular note is the evening departure of the North Sea Ferries, audible at least as far as Beverley High Road, and one of East Hull's pulses of time.

Estuarial happenings don't affect most people's lives over much, but the River Hull does. 'Bridge was up', again in the terse local vernacular, is fair excuse for lateness when meeting a friend, but not for more important appointments. Some East Hull drivers make detours between North and Drypool Bridges to try to keep on time — easy enough now there is less river traffic, but years ago it was a gamble, as a string of vessels could have both bridges up together or very quickly one after the other. Of course, trams and trolley buses could not make detours any more than river traffic can stop short to allow bridges to be put down. Now East and West are laced together across the dividing river by a succession of bridges, but, even so, road traffic must give way to the river. The new tunnel to provide a constant link is now under construction to the north of the city; to site one further south to bind East and West more closely together would be extremely costly and hardly practicable.

I write as an observer of the changing scene, so my choice of pictures has in part been dictated by those views of sufficient visual interest and thus there is no pictorial record of the Sutton Fields and the Citadel industrial estates, now forming important parts of Hull's industry and trade. They are collections of prefabricated boxes without any of the relieving features of a 'good' Victorian factory. Gardner, Barugh and Jones, however, kept a pediment of their former Waterhouse Lane premises as a frontispiece to their

Citadel works and a reminder of their long establishment. Traditional East Hull industries remain in much depleted form. Clarence Mill is the last representative of all the flour milling of the 19th century. Cargill's, upriver towards Stoneferry, is a major seed-crushing concern, producing rape and linseed oils. Humbrol and Seven Seas on Hedon Road, part of an inter-war attempt to position factories in more open situations and yet near to the docks, are producers of paints and vitamin supplements respectively, the latter a diversification from the original British Cod Liver Oil Products' fish oils and emulsions as providers of vitamins A and D. Engineering, started as an adjunct to milling and shipping, is still there in a variety of forms, Whittingham and Porter on the edge of the old Citadel site, being probably the oldest firm in this line, as Priestman's remains in name only.

The greatly improved road system has removed narrows and ugliness from Hedon, Holderness and Stoneferry Roads, but in places these main roads give the impression of unpopulated districts as there are so few pedestrians. The southern orbital road has taken some of the heavy traffic from the more residential outer ring road; Mount Pleasant, primarily for vehicles, not pedestrians, is pleasant in summer with the wild flowers, mayweed, and mellilot in particular, that have been allowed to flourish; the way to Stoneferry is transformed out of all recognition. Much of this change, however, was made possible by largescale bomb-damage, the removal of the railway and the demise of labour-intensive industry.

Though the air is cleaner, the shopping streets are not. For example, Holderness Road by late afternoon is covered with litter of all kinds, and, when the wind blows, no uncommon phenomenon hereabouts, papers, some sticky with food, polystyrene cartons and rattling drinks cans swirl about on the pavements. Sadly, this is a general disease, encountered not only in the eastern part of the city.

And yet... there are gardens between Field, Franklin and Brazil Streets, roses bloom in avenues off Redcar Street, vetches and other wild flowers grow in St. Mark Street, fields of beans drift their scent over North Bransholme and foxes bring their young near to the houses in Garden Village. Where there is work, most of it is more congenial than it used to be; all houses have been provided with decent facilities; there are swimming and sports at Ennerdale, the Woodford Centre and the old but refurbished East Hull Baths; there's a rugby team of no mean repute on Greatfield; a University of the Third Age meets at the former Ings Road School. It is just a short drive to Holland and Belgium via North Sea Ferries; over North Bridge and you are on the road to the seaside; hosts of golden daffodils brighten Holderness Road in the spring; there is a medieval church in Sutton and a stately home in Garden Village.... and more. Perhaps my perspective is not the same as yours, but, from where I'm standing, that's East Hull.

RAMSGATE CLOSE